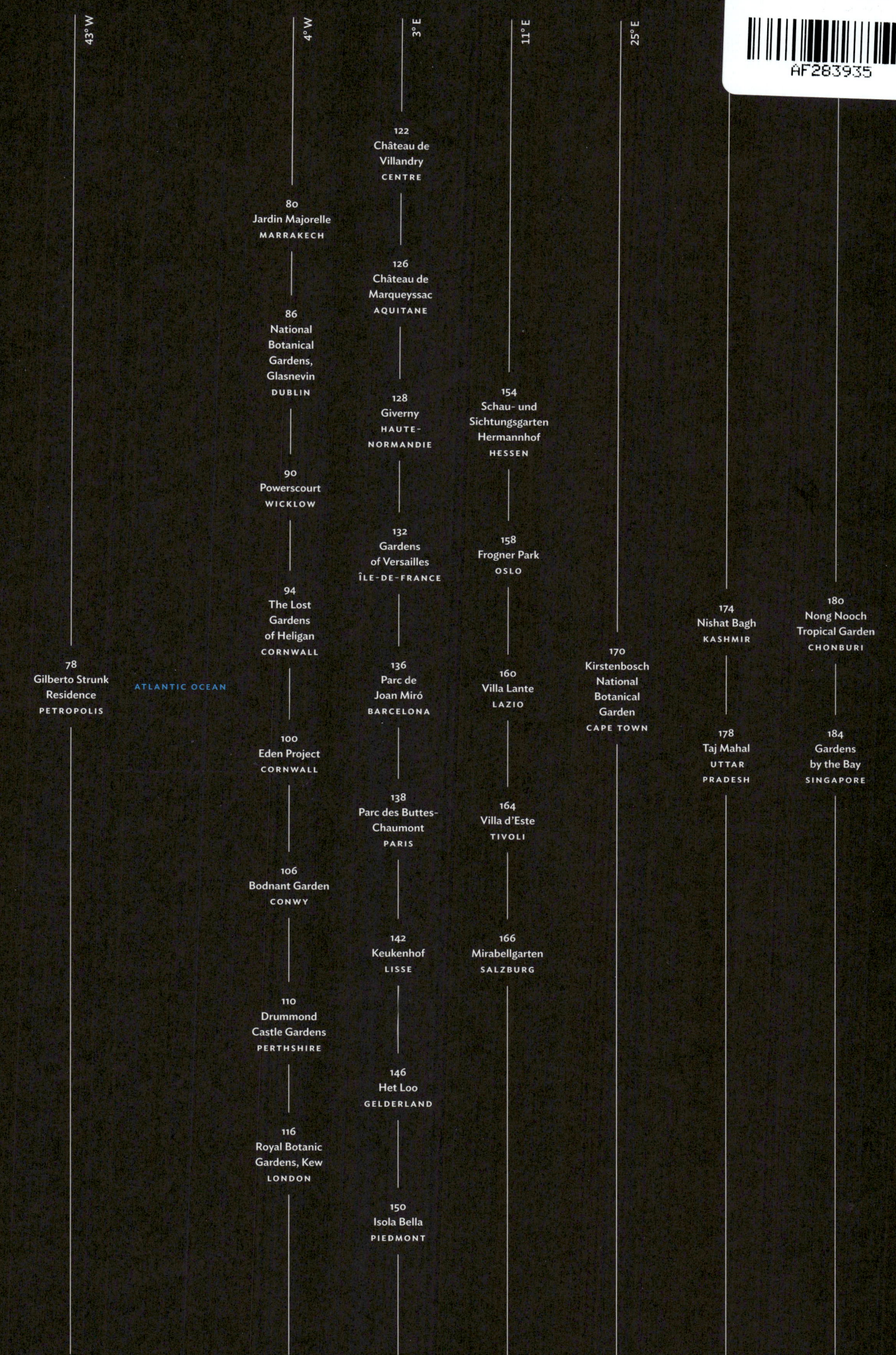

AF283935

43° W

4° W

3° E

11° E

25° E

122
Château de
Villandry
CENTRE

80
Jardin Majorelle
MARRAKECH

126
Château de
Marqueyssac
AQUITANE

86
National
Botanical
Gardens,
Glasnevin
DUBLIN

128
Giverny
HAUTE-
NORMANDIE

154
Schau- und
Sichtungsgarten
Hermannhof
HESSEN

90
Powerscourt
WICKLOW

132
Gardens
of Versailles
ÎLE-DE-FRANCE

158
Frogner Park
OSLO

94
The Lost
Gardens
of Heligan
CORNWALL

174
Nishat Bagh
KASHMIR

180
Nong Nooch
Tropical Garden
CHONBURI

78
Gilberto Strunk
Residence
PETROPOLIS

ATLANTIC OCEAN

136
Parc de
Joan Miró
BARCELONA

160
Villa Lante
LAZIO

170
Kirstenbosch
National
Botanical
Garden
CAPE TOWN

EAST

100
Eden Project
CORNWALL

178
Taj Mahal
UTTAR
PRADESH

184
Gardens
by the Bay
SINGAPORE

138
Parc des Buttes-
Chaumont
PARIS

164
Villa d'Este
TIVOLI

106
Bodnant Garden
CONWY

142
Keukenhof
LISSE

166
Mirabellgarten
SALZBURG

110
Drummond
Castle Gardens
PERTHSHIRE

146
Het Loo
GELDERLAND

116
Royal Botanic
Gardens, Kew
LONDON

150
Isola Bella
PIEDMONT

Roads Publishing
19–22 Dame Street
Dublin 2
Ireland

www.roads.co

First published 2015

1

Gardens
Roads Reflections
Text copyright © Roads Publishing
Design and layout copyright © Roads Publishing
Image copyright © the copyright holders; see p. 191
Design by Conor & David

Printed in India

British Library Cataloguing in Publication Data
A catalogue record for this book is available
from the British Library

Upper front-cover image:
Bodnant Garden
Lower front-cover image:
The Lost Gardens of Heligan
Back cover image:
Gardens by the Bay

978-1-909399-44-0

GARDENS

Foreword

Andrew Grant
Founder and Director, Grant Associates

'The Garden is a demonstration of thought.'
— Gilles Clément, *Guidelines for the Planetary Garden*

Gardens are an incomparable expression of human creativity and ingenuity. How many gardens must there be in the world? Millions, perhaps; each unique and specific to the geography, culture, economy and biodiversity present in their particular location on the planet. They also reflect the personal thoughts and ideas of each individual gardener, whether they are inspired by colour, hunger, conservation or comfort. Our fascination with gardens has been well documented through history, and there is great interest in the trends and changes in garden style that reflect each age.

While working on the Gardens by Bay in Singapore, I wondered how gardens of the twenty-first century would be remembered. What are the themes and issues that drive current garden creativity and what are the constants that have evolved through time? What inspires us to garden?

'[A garden] is a landscape whose combined vastness and definitiveness – whose united beauty, magnificence and strangeness, shall convey the idea of care, or culture, or superintendence.'
— Edgar Allan Poe

Although there are many ways to describe a garden, this is the definition that inspired our approach to designing Gardens by the Bay. Not only in regards to the beauty of gardens, but also their potential to evoke wonder and to create unknown experiences. In addition, gardens are artificial by their nature and depend on diligent and intelligent management and care. As well as the opportunity to create a visually and spatially spectacular garden experience – to be enjoyed during the tropical day and night – we saw the potential to develop an exemplary sustainable approach to the future of garden and park management in Singapore.

To design gardens one has to have the location and the future in mind. Of course, at the beginning we came at this project with an entirely Western perspective, and with only a cursory understanding of the Asian definition of gardens or indeed their cultures. In our client Dr Tan's analysis, our mindset was 'streamlined Scandinavian' rather than 'intricate Asian'. Over the period of the project we absorbed much of this intricate Asian thinking to create a richly detailed composite of garden culture and design. Much of this can be attributed to the special bond that developed between East and West, client and design team.

Never before had I experienced the complete sense of collaboration that forged these uniquely integrated gardens. This teamwork was, for me, one of the greatest memories of the project, which is really a story of how a group of individuals from different backgrounds, countries and interests came together to create one of the most striking landscape developments in the world.

Over 10 million people visited the Gardens in the first two years, each of them eager to experience the newness and the spectacular planting delivered by the Gardens by the Bay horticulture team. In fact the whole project is about plants. Specifically, to allow the full appreciation of their forms, colours, textures, functions, and, ultimately, their importance to us as humans in the twenty-first century. The Gardens by the Bay team sourced plants from across the planet to create a unique botanical reservoir and a visual and sensory spectacle. In addition to permanent planting displays and collections of rare species, the Gardens feature temporary displays and constant monitoring of plant growth and health, hence maintenance is an essential part of the story and is implicit in the client's desire to explore new boundaries in horticulture. The whole aspect of environmental sustainability was also a central theme of the design evolution, and involved going to considerable lengths to ensure an efficient energy strategy for the cooled conservatories, and the creation of

a unique reservoir of South-East Asian rainforest species. The core gardens are surrounded by a linked network of lakes and channels which form part of the water management for the site. This offers a water / wetland foreground to the Gardens and a linked network of filtration channels and storm attenuation, offering a working model of water-sensitive urban design. This combination of intelligent and sustainable environmental design, alongside the expression of wonder and delight, was a fundamental objective of the project and a combination that seems to me to be a prerequisite of any contemporary garden and landscape design.

At the heart of the Gardens are the Supertrees, which have quickly established themselves as the icons of the project. They are a rare fusion of design, nature and technology. They evoke science-fiction narratives and yet are tangible, enormous and expressive in scale, form and colour. We always saw the Supertrees as a counterpoint to the massive but beautiful conservatories, and they belong to the long tradition of extraordinary garden structures. Without the Supertrees the Gardens would just be about the conservatories with a series of gardens and planting attached. The Supertrees change the centre of gravity of Bay South and announce the true heart of the Gardens. Using the Supertrees, we wanted to create a centrepiece that became a fantastic tropical garden by day and a spectacular destination at night. At the same time, we wanted to make sure these structures delivered on many levels. They would be astonishing vertical tropical gardens, distinctive landmarks in the city, and would perform a number of important environmental services, including supporting photovoltaic panels, rainwater harvesting, hot air venting, exhaust fume venting and biodiversity habitat.

What is it that inspires such new ideas for gardens? In our work we are increasingly interested in referencing strong natural characteristics alongside technology and contemporary culture. The idea and feel for the Supertrees was in part inspired by the Valley of the Giants in Western Australia. I had visited these amazing trees when I went to see my brother who lives near Perth. The striking experience of changing from the normal eucalyptus forest into the super-tall world of the karri trees, along with the experience of the elevated walkway, was very inspiring. We merged this physical reference with the magical experience of the forest seen in the

In time, the true rainforest trees planted in the Gardens will reach the heights of these structures and become equal wonders of the project. Until then the Supertrees provide a unique skyline to the site and to the changing city context of Singapore.

Children are our future gardeners and I believe we have a duty to inspire them about the natural world but also to engage them with the art of growing and maintaining our future living world. At Gardens by the Bay, a sense of playfulness permeates the project but it is expressed most clearly in the Far East Organisation Children's Garden. Here, children are invited to explore physical challenges in the Forest Play and fun in the plant-inspired Water Play. In each case the contact with plants and natural phenomena is a central part of the play experience.

The completed project far exceeded the expectations of any of us who worked on it. The conservatories are spectacular and beautiful, the Supertrees are exotic and eccentric, the Gardens are a mosaic of intricacy and strangeness, and I really do believe the whole 54-hectare composition has a united beauty and magnificence that resonates with the idea of Singapore as a twenty-first-century city in a garden. We hope that this project does convey something to the wider world about the importance of beauty and wonder in our parks and gardens, the potential for integrated thinking to deliver a more environmentally sustainable future, and, above all, the power of imagination and trust that carried this extraordinary project through its many creative, political and economic battles to its remarkable physical manifestation.

Whilst the design and construction was completed just over two years ago, it is only the beginning of the life of the Gardens. This incredible collection of botanical diversity is still taking root and only hinting at the magnificence to come over the next 100 years and more. In time it is hoped that Bay South will mature into the living, breathing heart of this tropical metropolis, animated by generations of future residents of Singapore, visitors to this unique attraction and by the growing diversity of plants, animals, birds and insects that are already at home in this well-defined and beautifully maintained garden oasis.

It is hoped that Gardens by the Bay will be seen as the twenty-first-century counterpart to the many astonishing gardens that shaped the way we think about our shared green spaces, and that it will serve as an inspiration for future garden innovation.

Vorwort

„Der Garten ist eine Ausdrucksform des Gedankens."
— Gilles Clément, *Guidelines for the Planetary Garden (Leitfaden für den planetarischen Garten, Anm. d. Übers.)*

Gärten sind ein unvergleichlicher Ausdruck der menschlichen Kreativität und Genialität. Wie viele Gärten gibt es wohl auf der ganzen Welt? Vielleicht Millionen; jeder einzigartig und mit einem ganz spezifischen Bezug zur vorherrschenden Geografie, Wirtschaft und Biodiversität seines erdenweit einzigartigen Standortes. Darüber hinaus spiegeln Gärten auch die persönlichen Gedanken und Ideen der jeweiligen Gärtner, unabhängig davon, ob diese sich nun von Farben, Hunger, Umweltschutz oder Komfort inspirieren ließen. Unsere Faszination für Gärten ist historisch ausreichend belegt und noch immer rufen einzelne Trends und Veränderungen epochaler Gartenstile großes Interesse hervor.

Im Zuge meiner Arbeit an den „Gardens by the Bay" in Singapur stellte ich mir die Frage, wie man sich eines Tages wohl an die Gärten des 21. Jahrhunderts erinnern würde. Welche Themen und Fragestellungen speisen die gegenwärtige Gartenkreativität und welche Konstanten haben sich mit der Zeit herausgebildet? Was regt uns zum Gärtnern an?

„ [Ein Garten] ist eine Landschaft, deren kombinierte Weite und Endgültigkeit – deren kombinierte Schönheit, Pracht und Eigentümlichkeit die Idee von Sorgfalt, Kultur und Beaufsichtigung vermittelt. "
— Edgar Allan Poe

Obwohl sich ein Garten auf unterschiedlichste Art und Weise beschreiben lässt, lag unserem Entwurf für die „Gardens by the Bay" eben diese Definition zugrunde. Nicht nur was die Schönheit von Gärten anbelangt, sondern auch hinsichtlich ihres Potenzials, in Staunen zu versetzen und unbekannte Erfahrungen zu vermitteln. Darüber hinaus sind Gärten von Natur aus künstlich und von sorgfältiger und intelligenter Verwaltung und Pflege abhängig. Zusätzlich zur Chance, ein sowohl optisch als auch räumlich spektakuläres Erlebnis zu verwirklichen – das Tag und Nacht zu tropischem Genießen einlädt – sahen wir das Potenzial, einen ebenso beispielhaften wie nachhaltigen Zugang zur zukünftigen Garten- und Parkverwaltung in Singapur zu entwickeln.

Um Gärten zu entwerfen, gilt es, den Standort und die zukünftige Entwicklung zu bedenken. Es verwundert nicht, dass wir anfangs mit einer vollkommen westlichen Perspektive an dieses Projekt herangingen, sowie einem lediglich oberflächlichen Verständnis der asiatischen Definition von Gärten bzw. ihrer Kulturen. Unserem Auftraggeber Dr. Tan zufolge, war unsere Denkweise überwiegend „stromlinienförmig skandinavisch" statt „verschlungen asiatisch". Im Laufe dieses Projekts übernahmen wir dann aber doch einen Gutteil dieser verschlungenen asiatischen Denkart, um ein detailreiches Gemenge aus Gartenkultur und -design zu entwerfen. Vieles davon lässt sich der einzigartigen Verbindung zuschreiben, die sich zwischen Ost und West, zwischen dem Auftraggeber und dem Entwurfsteam entwickelte.

Nie zuvor hatte ich dieses vollkommene Gefühl der Zusammenarbeit erlebt, das diese einzigartigen ganzheitlichen Gärten ermöglichte. Zu den schönsten Erinnerungen rund um dieses Projekt zählt für mich gerade diese Form des Teamworks, bei dem es sich in Wahrheit um die Geschichte einer Gruppe aus Individuen handelt, die zwar durch unterschiedliche Hintergründe, Länder und Interessen geprägt waren, die jedoch einen Augenblick lang an einem Strang zogen, um eines der beeindruckendsten Landschaftsentwicklungprojekte der Welt zu realisieren.

Über 10 Millionen Menschen haben diese Gärten in den ersten beiden Jahren bereits besucht, begierig darauf, die Neuheit zu erleben sowie die spektakulären Pflanzungen zu bewundern, die von den Gartenbauern der „Gardens by the Bay" angelegt wurden. Tatsächlich dreht sich das gesamte Projekt um Pflanzen. Insbesondere darum, die uneingeschränkte Wertschätzung ihrer Formen, Farben, Texturen, Funktionen und letztendlich ihrer Bedeutung für uns Menschen im 21. Jahrhundert zu ermöglichen. Das „Gardens by the Bay"-Team beschaffte Pflanzen aus aller Herren Länder,

Avant-propos

« Le jardin est la démonstration d'une pensée »
— Gilles Clément, *Approche du jardin planétaire*

Les jardins sont l'expression remarquable de la créativité et de l'ingéniosité des hommes. Combien de jardins compte la planète ? Des millions, sans doute ; autant de jardins dont la singularité tient à la géographie, à la culture, à l'économie ou encore à la biodiversité particulière de leur emplacement dans le globe. Ils traduisent également l'état d'esprit et les idées personnelles du jardinier, à la faveur d'inspirations esthétiques ou de motivations potagères, de missions de conservation ou de questions de bien-être. Au fil des courants et des évolutions stylistiques propres à chaque époque, l'histoire montre à quel point les jardins ont toujours fasciné les hommes.

Quel témoignage laisseront les jardins du vingt-et-unième siècle ? Tel a été le fil conducteur qui a dirigé les travaux du projet des Gardens by the Bay à Singapour. A quelles thématiques et problématiques répond la créativité des jardins d'aujourd'hui ? Quelles sont les constantes qui se dégagent dans le temps ? De quelle inspiration se nourrit l'art paysager ?

« [Un jardin] est un paysage où la vastitude et la délimitation habilement combinées, où la réunion de la beauté, de la magnificence et de l'étrangeté, suggèreront l'idée de soins, de cultures et de surintendance ».
— Edgar Allan Poe

S'il existe mille et une façons de décrire un jardin, c'est bien la définition que l'on peut en donner qui a inspiré notre approche des Gardens by the Bay dont l'aménagement aspire à reproduire la beauté des jardins, mais aussi à traduire tout le potentiel d'évocation qu'ils renferment, entre merveilles et expériences inédites. En outre, les jardins relèvent par définition de l'artificiel et dépendent de soins et d'une gestion réactive et intelligente. Outre la possibilité de proposer aux visiteurs une expérience du jardin spectaculaire tant sur le plan visuel que spatial – à vivre de jour comme de nuit sous le climat tropical de Singapour – l'opportunité d'adopter une approche de développement durable exemplaire visant à assurer la pérennité du jardin et sa gestion responsable s'est naturellement imposée.

Un jardin ne peut se concevoir sans avoir à l'esprit son implantation et son avenir. Bien sûr, nous avons commencé par appréhender ce projet dans une perspective purement occidentale avec une connaissance somme toute sommaire de la manière dont les Asiatiques définissent les jardins, ou tout simplement de leur culture. Notre client, le Dr Tan, a très bien résumé notre état d'esprit qu'il jugeait davantage ancré dans un « rationalisme scandinave » que dans la « subtilité asiatique ». A mesure que progressait le projet, nous nous sommes imprégnés de cette subtile pensée asiatique pour créer une véritable culture et un aménagement paysager aux compositions aussi riches que variées. Un travail essentiellement rendu possible grâce à ce lien spécial entre Orient et Occident, que l'équipe de conception a noué avec le client.

Mon expérience personnelle de la collaboration n'a jamais pris autant de sens que dans le cadre de ces jardins dont l'intégration a été exceptionnelle. Ce travail d'équipe fut pour moi l'un des meilleurs souvenirs du projet, et illustre à merveille la manière dont un groupe composé de plusieurs individus issus de milieux et de pays différents et aux intérêts divers a uni ses forces pour développer un paysage parmi les plus remarquables du monde.

Durant leurs deux premières années d'existence, les Jardins ont accueilli plus de 10 millions de visiteurs, chacun désireux de goûter à la nouveauté et d'apprécier la végétation spectaculaire mise en scène par l'équipe horticole des Gardens by the Bay. Car, le projet tout entier est consacré aux plantes, dans le but précis d'en faire pleinement apprécier les formes, les couleurs, les textures, les fonctions et enfin de souligner leur importance pour nous, humains du vingt-et-unième siècle. L'équipe des Gardens by the Bay a fait venir des espèces des quatre

Prólogo

«El jardín es la demostración de un pensamiento.»
— Gilles Clément, *Approche du jardin planétaire*

Los jardines constituyen una expresión incomparable de la creatividad y la inventiva humanas. ¿Cuántos jardines puede haber en el mundo? Quizá, millones; cada uno de ellos único y específico de la geografía, la cultura, la economía y la biodiversidad existentes en su lugar del planeta. Representan igualmente el reflejo de los pensamientos e ideas personales de los jardineros en su individualidad, ya basen su inspiración en el color, el hambre, la conservación o el confort. Nuestra fascinación por los jardines aparece bien documentada a lo largo de la historia, así como el gran interés por las tendencias y los cambios en el estilo de los jardines, que son el reflejo de cada época.

Mientras trabajaba en los Gardens by the Bay de Singapur, me preguntaba qué se recordaría de los jardines del siglo XXI. ¿Cuáles son los temas y las cuestiones que impulsan la creatividad actual de los jardines y cuáles las constantes que han evolucionado a lo largo del tiempo? ¿Qué nos impulsa a crear jardines?

« [Un jardín] es un paisaje cuya inmensidad y limitación combinadas, cuya belleza, magnificencia y rareza reunidas transmiten la idea de cuidado, de cultura y de suprema dirección.»
— Edgar Allan Poe

Aunque un jardín se puede describir de infinitas maneras, ésta es la definición que inspiró nuestro planteamiento a la hora de diseñar los Gardens by the Bay, no solo en lo que respecta a la belleza de los jardines, sino también su capacidad para provocar fascinación y suscitar experiencias ignoradas. Los jardines, artificiales por naturaleza, dependen de una gestión y un cuidado diligentes e inteligentes. Además de la oportunidad de crear una experiencia de jardín espectacular, tanto en lo visual como lo espacial, para su disfrute en los días y noches tropicales, vimos la posibilidad de desarrollar un planteamiento sostenible ejemplar para el futuro de los parques y jardines de Singapur.

Para diseñar jardines, uno debe tener el espacio y el futuro en mente. Por supuesto, al principio llegamos a este proyecto con una perspectiva totalmente occidental y solo con un entendimiento superficial de lo que significaban en Asia los jardines o incluso de sus culturas. Según el análisis de nuestro cliente, el Dr. Tan, nuestro modo de pensar era «escandinavo funcional» en lugar de «asiático intrincado». A lo largo de todo el proyecto, fuimos absorbiendo buena parte de este pensamiento asiático intrincado y terminamos creando una combinación detallada y compleja de la cultura y el diseño de jardines. En gran medida, esto se puede atribuir al vínculo especial que surgió entre Oriente y Occidente, entre el cliente y el equipo de diseño.

Nunca antes había experimentado yo una sensación tan entera de colaboración, gracias a la cual se forjaron estos jardines perfectamente integrados. Creo que uno de mis mejores recuerdos del proyecto fue el equipo de trabajo: cómo un grupo de personas de distintos orígenes, países e intereses se unieron para hacer realidad una de las creaciones paisajísticas más sorprendentes del mundo.

Más de 10 millones de personas visitaron los Jardines los dos primeros años, todas ellas dispuestas a experimentar la novedad y la espectacular plantación creada por el equipo de horticultura de los Gardens by the Bay. De hecho, todo el proyecto gira en torno a las plantas. De un modo más concreto, se trata de poder apreciar sus formas, colores, texturas, funciones y, por último, de resaltar su importancia para nosotros los humanos del siglo XXI. Gracias al equipo de los Gardens by the Bay, que consiguió plantas de todo el planeta, se ha podido crear una reserva botánica única y todo un espectáculo visual y sensorial. Además de los despliegues y las colecciones de plantaciones permanentes de especies raras, los Jardines presentan despliegues temporales. Así, la importancia vital del mantenimiento se refleja en la constante supervisión del estado y el crecimiento de las plantas. El deseo del cliente lleva igualmente implícito

um so einen einzigartigen botanischen Speicher sowie ein optisches und sinnliches Spektakel zu erschaffen. Zusätzlich zu permanenten Pflanzungen und Sammlungen seltener Spezies bieten die Gärten außerdem vorübergehende Schauen und ermöglichen das fortwährende Beobachten von Pflanzenwachstum und –gesundheit, was zeigt, welch entscheidende Rolle der Erhaltung in dieser Geschichte zukommt, die dem Wunsch des Auftraggebers zugrunde liegt, neue Gartenbaugrenzen auszuloten. Der gesamte Aspekt der umweltgerechten Nachhaltigkeit stand dann auch im Zentrum der Entwurfsentwicklung, was dazu führte, dass keinerlei Mühen gescheut wurden, um eine effiziente Energiestrategie für die gekühlten Gewächshäuser sicherzustellen, und die Schaffung eines einzigartigen Refugiums für südostasiatische Regelwaldarten bewirkte. Das Innere der Gärten ist umgeben von einem verbundenen Netzwerk aus Seen und Kanälen, die Teil der Wasserbewirtschaftung dieses Standortes sind. Auf diese Weise entsteht eine wasserreiche Auenlandschaft im Vordergrund zu den Gärten sowie ein Geflecht aus Sickermulden, die nicht nur die Auswirkungen von Tropenstürmen abschwächen, sondern zudem ein leistungsfähiges, das Element Wasser miteinbeziehendes urbanes Designmodell bieten. Neben dem Aspekt des Staunenmachens bzw. Entzückens handelt es sich bei dieser Verbindung aus intelligentem und nachhaltigem Umweltdesign um eines der grundlegenden Ziele des Projekts und meiner Ansicht nach um eine Grundvoraussetzung für jede zeitgenössische Garten- und Landschaftsgestaltung.

Das Herzstück des Gartens bilden die sogenannten „Superbäume", die binnen kürzester Zeit zum Symbol dieses Projekts avancierten und eine einzigartige Verschmelzung von Design, Natur und Technologie bilden. Wiewohl sie an Science-Fiction-Geschichten denken lassen, sind sie doch greifbar, gewaltig und ausdrucksstark in ihrer Größe, Form und Färbung. Wir haben diese Superbäume stets als Kontrapunkt zu den atemberaubenden Gewächshäusern verstanden, die untrennbar mit der langen Tradition außerordentlicher Gartenstrukturen verbunden sind. Ohne die Superbäume ginge es in diesem Garten lediglich um die von zahlreichen Pflanzungen umgebenen Gewächshäuser. Die Superbäume verändern den Schwerpunkt der südlichen Bucht und künden vom tatsächlichen Wahrzeichen dieser Gärten. Mit der Einbeziehung der Superbäume beabsichtigten wir, ein prunkvolles Kernstück zu erschaffen, das tagsüber ein fantastischer Tropengarten und des nachts ein atemberaubender Publikumsmagnet sein würde. Gleichzeitig wollten wir sicherstellen, dass diese Strukturen auf mehreren Ebenen zu beeindrucken wissen; sie sollten nicht nur als erstaunliche vertikale Tropengärten oder markante Wahrzeichen der Stadt fungieren, sondern auch eine ganze Reihe wichtiger Umweltfunktionen erfüllen, wie beispielsweise Fotovoltaikanlagen zu beherbergen, Regenwasser zu sammeln, heiße Luftmassen sowie Abgase abzuleiten und als Hort der Biodiversität zu dienen.

Was aber führt zu solch neuen Gartenideen? Bei unserer Arbeit war uns mehr und mehr daran gelegen, Bezüge zwischen starken natürlichen Charakteristika und Technologie einserseits bzw. zeitgenössischer Kultur andererseits herzustellen. Die Idee und das Gefühl für die Superbäume wurden uns teilweise vom westaustralischen „Tal der Giganten" eingegeben. Ich habe mir diese erstaunlichen Bäume angeshen als ich meinem Bruder einen Besuch abstattete, der unweit von Perth lebt. Das eindrucksvolle Erlebnis des Übergangs vom herkömmlichen Eukalyptuswald hinüber in die Riesen welt der Karribäume, ergänzt um die Erfahrung des Wipfelwanderwegs, hat mich tief berührt. Wir verbanden bei der Festlegung der Eigenschaften und Größe des Supertree Grove („Hain der Superbäume", Anm. d. Übers.) diesen physischen Bezug mit dem magischen Walderlebnis aus dem Film *Prinzessin Mononoke* des Studio Ghibli.

Mit der Zeit werden die hier gepflanzten echten Regenwaldbäume die verschiedenen Höhen der einzelnen Strukturen erreichen und im Rahmen dieses Projekts zu gleichberechtigten Wundern heranwachsen. Bis dahin sorgen die Superbäume für eine einzigartige Skyline des Ortes sowie des sich fortwährend wandelnden Stadtkontextes von Singapur. Kinder sind die zukünftigen Gärtner und ich glaube, dass wir

coins du monde pour constituer ce réservoir botanique unique à contempler et à ressentir. Outre les aménagements végétaux permanents et les collections d'espèces rares, les Jardins abritent également des expositions temporaires et assurent la surveillance constante de la croissance des plantes et de leur bien-être. Composante essentielle du développement des Jardins, l'entretien s'impose naturellement dans le souhait du client d'explorer l'horticulture au-delà des limites conventionnelles. Autre thématique centrale dans le cheminement conceptuel des Jardins, l'aspect global du développement durable dans l'environnement a mobilisé des efforts considérables pour assurer le refroidissement des serres à travers une stratégie énergétique efficace, et créer un réservoir unique d'espèces tropicales d'Asie du Sud-Est. Les jardins centraux sont ainsi entourés d'un réseau croisé de bassins et de canaux parfaitement intégrés à la gestion de l'eau du site. Ce réseau constitue une réserve d'eau/d'humidité de premier plan pour les jardins, que complète le système croisé de canaux de filtration et de réduction des eaux de ruissellement, pour fournir un modèle opérationnel d'aménagement urbain soucieux de la gestion de l'eau. Cette conception environnementale alliant bon sens et durabilité, au-delà de l'émerveillement et du ravissement qu'elle suscite, a constitué l'objectif fondamental du projet. Une combinaison préalable selon moi à toute conception de jardins et de paysages contemporains.

En plein cœur des jardins culminent les arbres géants baptisés « Supertrees », qui sont rapidement devenus l'emblème du projet. Alliance singulière entre architecture, nature et technologie, ils confèrent aux jardins une allure futuriste, et ce malgré des dimensions et des formes concrètes hors normes et imposantes dans des couleurs expressives. Les Supertrees s'inscrivent en contrepoint des serres certes magnifiques, mais massives, et puisent leur source dans la longue tradition des structures du jardin extraordinaire. Sans eux, les jardins se résumeraient à un alignement de serres dans une suite de parcs et d'espaces arborés. Les Supertrees modifient véritablement le centre de gravité de Bay South en préfigurant le véritable cœur des jardins. Avec ces arbres géants, nous avons voulu composer une pièce maîtresse, tour à tour jardin tropical fantastique le jour et fabuleuse attraction la nuit. Nous souhaitions dans le même temps des structures multifonctionnelles qui feraient à la fois office de jardins tropicaux verticaux à couper le souffle et de repères distinctifs de la ville, tout en offrant un certain nombre de services environnementaux non négligeables, comme abriter des panneaux photovoltaïques, récupérer les eaux de pluie, ventiler l'air chaud, évacuer les gaz d'échappement et offrir un habitat à la biodiversité.

Dans quelle source d'inspiration puiser de nouvelles idées pour les jardins ? Nos travaux nous incitent toujours plus à référencer les propriétés naturelles pérennes aux côtés de la culture technologique et contemporaine. Le concept des Supertrees et l'impression qu'ils procurent ont été en partie inspirés par la Vallée des Géants en Australie occidentale. J'ai pu contempler ces arbres incroyables lors d'un séjour chez mon frère, près de Perth. Passer d'une forêt d'eucalyptus traditionnelle au monde géant des arbres karris à bord d'une passerelle a été une expérience particulièrement inspirante. Avec mon équipe, nous avons fusionné ce site naturel avec l'image enchanteresse de la forêt imaginée par le Studio Ghibli dans le film d'animation japonais *Princesse Mononoké* pour conférer à la forêt de Supertrees son caractère et son échelle si particulière.

Avec le temps, les vrais arbres tropicaux plantés dans les Jardins rivaliseront avec la hauteur de ces structures pour devenir les futures merveilles du projet. En attendant, les Supertrees offrent une ligne d'horizon unique au site, ainsi qu'au milieu urbain changeant de Singapour.

Les enfants sont les jardiniers de demain. Nous avons le devoir de leur inspirer le monde de la nature, et surtout de les encourager à développer et à entretenir le monde vivant de demain. Les Gardens by the Bay mettent à l'honneur les aspects ludiques qui transparaissent dans le projet, des aspects qui s'expriment de manière très claire dans le Far East Organisation Children's Garden (Jardin des enfants

la exploración de nuevos límites en la horticultura. La cuestión de la sostenibilidad medioambiental, en su conjunto, constituyó también un punto fundamental de la evolución del diseño: la disposición de una estrategia energética eficaz para los invernaderos refrigerados y la creación de una reserva única de especies de la selva tropical del sudeste asiático implicaron un esfuerzo considerable. Los jardines principales están rodeados de una red interconectada de lagos y canales que forman parte de la gestión de las aguas del emplazamiento. Esto ofrece una base de aguas y humedales a los jardines y una red interconectada de canales de filtración y atenuación de tormentas, que proporciona un modelo de trabajo en lo que a diseños urbanos sensibles al agua se refiere. Esta combinación de diseño medioambiental inteligente y sostenible, junto con la expresión de fascinación y delicia, constituía un objetivo fundamental del proyecto, todo ello requisito indispensable, creo yo, para cualquier diseño paisajístico y de jardín contemporáneo.

En el centro de los jardines, los Superárboles se proclamaron rápidamente los iconos del proyecto. Constituyen una fusión poco común de diseño, naturaleza y tecnología. Evocación de los relatos de ciencia ficción, siguen siendo a la vez tangibles, enormes y expresivos en su escala, forma y color. Siempre hemos considerado los Superárboles como contrapunto a los invernaderos, espléndidos aunque enormes. Forman parte de una larga tradición de estructuras extraordinarias en los jardines. Sin los Superárboles, estos jardines estarían formados solo por los invernaderos con una serie de jardines y plantaciones adyacentes. Son ellos los que modifican el centro de gravedad de Bay South y anuncian el verdadero centro de los jardines. Los Superárboles nos han ayudado a crear un centro de mesa que se convierte en un jardín tropical fantástico de día y en un destino espectacular de noche. Al mismo tiempo, queríamos asegurarnos de que estas estructuras cumplían sus numerosos objetivos: ser unos asombrosos jardines tropicales verticales, resaltar como hitos característicos de la ciudad y ofrecer algunos servicios medioambientales importantes, como el sostenimiento de paneles fotovoltaicos, la recogida de aguas pluviales, la salida de aire caliente, la evacuación de tubos de escape y como hábitat de la biodiversidad.

¿En qué se inspiran estas nuevas ideas para los jardines? En nuestra profesión, nos sentimos cada vez más motivados por tener en cuenta características naturales poderosas, así como la tecnología y la cultura contemporánea. La idea y la impresión que transmiten los Superárboles procede en parte del Valle de los Gigantes, en Australia Occidental. Visité estos sorprendentes árboles al ir a ver a mi hermano que vive cerca de Perth. La asombrosa experiencia de pasar de un bosque de eucaliptos normal al mundo gigantesco de los árboles de karri, además de la sorprendente pasarela elevada, fueron realmente inspiradoras. Fusionamos esta referencia física con la experiencia mágica del bosque que aparece en la película La Princesa Mononoke de Studio Ghibli para crear el estilo y el tamaño del Bosque de Superárboles.

Con el tiempo, los verdaderos árboles de la selva tropical plantados en los Jardines alcanzarán la misma altura que estas estructuras y se convertirán igualmente en otra de las maravillas de este proyecto. Hasta entonces, los Superárboles proporcionarán una línea del horizonte singular a este paraje y al cambiante paisaje de la ciudad de Singapur.

Los niños son nuestros jardineros del mañana y creo que tenemos el deber de motivarles sobre el mundo natural, así como de iniciarles en el arte de cultivar y conservar el mundo de los seres vivos del futuro. En los Gardens by the Bay, una sensación lúdica impregna todo el proyecto, pero se expresa con mayor claridad en el jardín de los niños Far East Organisation Children's Garden. Aquí, se anima a los niños a superar desafíos físicos en el Forest Play y a divertirse en el Water Play, de clara inspiración vegetal. En ambos casos, el contacto con las plantas y los fenómenos naturales forman parte consustancial de la experiencia lúdica.

El proyecto finalizado superó con creces las expect ativas de todos los que participamos en él: espectaculares y magníficos invernaderos, exóticos y pintorescos Superárboles, y un mosaico de complejos y extraños jardines. Creo real-

die Aufgabe haben, ihnen die Faszination für den Naturraum zu vermitteln, sie aber auch die Kunst des Pflanzens und Erhaltens unserer hinkünftigen Umwelt zu lehren. Bei „Gardens by the Bay" durchweht ein Hauch von Verspieltheit das ganze Projekt, die wohl am deutlichsten von der fernöstlichen Organisation „Children's Garden" zum Ausdruck gebracht wird. Diese fordert Kinder dazu auf, sich im Rahmen des „Forest Play" körperlichen Herausforderungen zu stellen und im von Pflanzen inspirierten „Water Play" Spaß zu haben. In beiden Fällen bildet der Kontakt zu Pflanzen und Naturphänomenen das Herzstück der spielerischen Erlebniswelt.

Das vollendete Projekt übertraf sämtliche Erwartungen aller daran beteiligten Personen um ein Vielfaches. Die Gewächshäuser sind atemberaubend und wunderschön, die Superbäume exotisch und exzentrisch, die Gärten bilden ein verschlungenes und eigentümliches Mosaik und ich bin aufrichtig von der kombinierten Schönheit und Herrlichkeit der 54 Hektar großen Komposition überzeugt, die vom Singapur des 21. Jahrhunderts als einer Stadt inmitten von Gärten kündet. Wir hoffen, dass dieses Projekt der übrigen Welt etwas über die Bedeutung von Schönheit und Faszination in unseren Parks und Gärten vermittelt, über das Potenzial integrierten Denkens hinsichtlich einer umweltfreundlicheren und nachhaltigeren Zukunft sowie, allen voran, über die Kraft der Vorstellung und des Vertrauens, denen es zu verdanken ist, dass dieses außergewöhnliche Projekt trotz aller kreativen, politischen und wirtschaftlichen Schwierigkeiten umgesetzt werden konnte.

Während der Entwurf und die Ausführung bereits vor zwei Jahren vollendet werden konnten, steckt dieser Garten nach wie vor in den Kinderschuhen. Diese unglaubliche Sammlung botanischer Diversität, die ihre Pracht der kommenden 100 und mehr Jahre nur ansatzweise erahnen lässt, muss diesen erst noch entwachsen. Mit der Zeit wird sich die Südbucht hoffentlich in das lebendige und schlagende Herz der Tropenmetropole Singapur wandeln, und von Generationen zukünftiger Stadtbewohner aufgesucht werden, die von der einzigartigen Anziehungskraft und der wachsenden Diversität der Pflanzen, Tiere, Vögel und Insekten dieses Ortes angezogen werden, deren Zuhause die klar definierte und hübsch erhaltene Gartenoase bereits heute ist.

Es besteht die Hoffnung, dass die „Gardens by the Bay" das moderne Gegenstück zu den zahlreichen erstaunlichen Gärten bilden werden, die unsere Wahrnehmung gemeinschaftlicher Grünflächen beeinflusst haben, und als Inspirationsquelle für zukünftige Garteninnovationen dienen werden.

de l'Organisation d'Extrême-Orient). Là, les enfants sont invités à relever des défis physiques dans le Forest Play (aire de jeux en forêt), et à s'amuser dans le Water Play (jeux d'eau) inspiré par les plantes. Dans chaque cas, le contact avec les plantes et les phénomènes naturels joue un rôle central dans l'expérience ludique.

Le projet achevé a largement dépassé les attentes de chacun de ses concepteurs. Les serres sont aussi spectaculairement que magnifiques, et les Supertrees aussi exotiques qu'originaux, avec pour écrin des Jardins formant une véritable mosaïque aussi sophistiquée que curieuse. Les 54 hectares de cette vaste composition se distinguent par une beauté réellement harmonieuse et une magnificence qui entre en résonance avec l'idée de Singapour incarnant la ville-jardin du vingt-et-unième siècle. Ce projet aspire à transmettre au monde entier sa vision axée sur l'importance de la beauté et de l'émerveillement que suscitent nos parcs et nos jardins, sur la possibilité d'intégrer la réflexion à la construction d'un avenir plus durable sur le plan environnemental, et surtout, sur le pouvoir de l'imagination et la confiance qui ont permis de mener de front les nombreux défis créatifs, politiques et économiques de ce projet extraordinaire jusqu'à lui donner vie dans son expression physique incomparable.

Si la conception et la construction du projet se sont achevées il y a tout juste deux ans, les Jardins ne sont qu'à l'aube de leur vie. Cette incroyable collection de diversité botanique prend encore racine et n'atteindra sa véritable splendeur que d'ici les 100 années à venir, voire au-delà. Bay South devrait au fil du temps devenir un poumon vivant et dynamique de la métropole tropicale, sous l'impulsion des futures générations de Singapouriens, visiteurs de cette attraction unique, et de la diversité croissante de la faune (animaux, oiseaux et insectes) et de la flore déjà chez elles dans cette oasis végétale parfaitement définie et merveilleusement entretenue.

Notre souhait le plus cher est que les Gardens by the Bay incarnent le jardin du vingt-et-unième siècle au même titre que les nombreux autres jardins surprenants qui ont façonné notre conception des espaces verts partagés, et inspirent les nouveaux jardins de demain.

mente que toda la composición de 54 hectáreas presenta una unidad de belleza y magnificencia, que se refleja en la idea de que Singapur es una ciudad del siglo XXI en medio de un jardín. Deseamos que este proyecto transmita algo al resto del mundo sobre la importancia de la belleza y la fascinación en nuestros parques y jardines, sobre la capacidad de ofrecer un future medioambientalmente sostenible mediante una reflexión global y, por encima de todo, sobre el poder de la imaginación y la confianza que impulsaron a este extraordinario proyecto, tras intensas luchas creativas, políticas y económicas, hasta su extraordinaria materialización.

Aunque el diseño y la construcción finalizaron hace dos años, esto solo es el principio de la vida de los Jardines. Esta increíble recopilación de diversidad botánica sigue echando raíces e insinúa apenas la magnificencia que mostrará en los próximos 100 años y más allá. Con el tiempo, se espera que Bay South madure hasta convertirse en el corazón viviente de esta metrópolis tropical, animado por generaciones de futuros residentes de Singapur, visitantes de esta singular atracción, y por la creciente diversidad de plantas, animales, aves e insectos que ya han hecho su hogar de este oasis ajardinado magníficamente delimitado y conservado.

Esperamos que los Gardens by the Bay se consideren como la contrapartida del siglo XXI a muchos de los sorprendentes jardines que han dado forma a nuestro modo de pensar sobre los espacios verdes compartidos y que sirvan de inspiración para la innovación de futuros jardines.

Yu Yuan
Shanghai, China

This classical Chinese garden, situated beside the City God Temple in the north-east of the old city of Shanghai, does justice to the name 'Yu', which can be translated as 'pleasing' or 'enjoyable'. The history of the garden can be traced back more than four hundred years to the Ming Dynasty, when an official, Pan Yunduan, had the garden made for the enjoyment of his retired father. It has undergone many changes since this period, especially when it was severely damaged in the nineteenth century during the Opium Wars. However, Yu Yuan, with its pavilions, halls, rockeries, ponds and cloisters, is still a treasure to behold for the modern visitor.

Dieser klassische chinesiche Garten befindet sich unmittelbar neben dem Stadtgotttempel im Nordosten der Shanghaier Altstadt, und macht seinem Namen alle Ehre, heißt „Yu" doch so viel wie „erfreulich" bzw. „angenehm". Die Geschichte dieser Grünanlage lässt sich über mehr als vier Jahrhunderte bis zur Ming-Dynastie zurückverfolgen, als ein hoher Beamter namens Pan Yunduan diesen Garten errichten ließ, um seinem pensionierten Vater eine Freude zu machen. Seither hat sich der Yu Yuan mehrmals gehörig verändert, insbesondere im 19. Jahrhundert anlässlich seiner Beschädigung während des Opiumkrieges. Nichtsdestotrotz stellt der Yu-Yuan-Garten mit seinen Pavillons, Hallen, Steingärten, Teichen und Laubengängen für moderne Besucher auch heute noch ein wahres Kleinod dar.

Ce jardin classique chinois, situé à côté du Temple du Dieu de la ville au nord-est de la vieille ville de Shanghai, rend effectivement justice au terme « Yu », que l'on peut traduire par « plaisant » ou « agréable ». L'histoire de ce jardin remonte à plus de quatre cents ans à l'époque de la dynastie Ming, lorsqu'un officiel de haut rang, Pan Yunduan, décida d'aménager un jardin pour le plaisir de son père à la retraite. Le jardin a connu de nombreuses transformations depuis, notamment après avoir été gravement endommagé pendant la Guerre de l'opium au dix-neuvième siècle. Pour autant, Yuyuan, avec ses pavillons, ses corridors, ses rocailles, ses bassins et ses cloîtres, reste un véritable régal pour les yeux du visiteur moderne.

Yu Yuan, Shanghai, China

Este clásico jardín chino, situado junto al Templo del Dios de la Ciudad, en el noreste del casco antiguo de Shanghai, hace justicia al nombre «Yu», que se puede traducir por «grato» o «placentero». La historia del jardín puede remontarse más de cuatrocientos años hasta la dinastía Ming, cuando un funcionario, Pan Yunduan, mandó construir el jardín para el disfrute de su padre retirado. Ha experimentado numerosos cambios desde ese período, especialmente, cuando sufrió graves daños durante las Guerras del Opio, en el siglo XIX. No obstante, Yu Yuan, con sus pabellones, salas, rocallas, estanques y claustros, sigue siendo un tesoro digno de ser admirado por los actuales visitantes.

Changdeokgung
Seoul, South Korea

Changdeokgung, Seoul, South Korea

The royal palace of Changdeokgung dates back to 1405 and is now listed as a UNESCO World Heritage site. The Piwon or 'secret garden' hidden within its walls was designed in the traditional natural landscape fashion and was for the exclusive use of the royal family and the king's concubines during the Joseon Dynasty. The garden incorporates a lotus pond, pavilions, elegant stone bridges, landscaped lawns and a 700-year-old juniper tree. The pavilion, at one time, housed a royal library and was a place where king and courtiers studied and discussed politics.

Der königliche Palast von Changdeokgung geht auf das Jahr 1405 zurück und ist Teil des UNESCO-Weltkulturerbes. Der innerhalb der Mauern verborgene Piwon oder „Geheime Garten" wurde entsprechend der traditionellen natürlichen Landschaftsgestaltung angelegt und stand während der Joseon-Dynastie ausschließlich der königlichen Familie sowie den Konkubinen des Königs zur Verfügung. Der Garten lockt mit einem Lotus-Teich, Pavillons, eleganten Steinbrücken, kunstvoll gestalteten Rasenflächen und einem 700 Jahre alten Wacholderbaum. Einst beherbergte der Pavillon eine königliche Bibliothek und diente dem Herrscher und seinen Höflingen als Studierzimmer sowie für politische Debatten.

La construction du palais royal Changdeokgung remonte à 1405. Le palais
figure aujourd'hui au patrimoine
mondial de l'UNESCO. Le « jardin secret »
ou Piwon qu'il dissimule dans son
enceinte a été conçu dans la plus
pure tradition du paysage naturel pour
l'usage exclusif de la famille royale et
des concubines du roi sous la dynastie
Joseon. On peut y admirer un étang
de lotus, des pavillons, d'élégants
ponts en pierre, des décors paysagers
et un genévrier vieux de 700 ans.
Le pavillon a pendant un temps abrité
la bibliothèque royale où le roi et ses
courtisans venaient se cultiver et
débattre de politique.

El palacio real de Changdeokgung se remonta a 1405 y actualmente está declarado Patrimonio de la Humanidad de la UNESCO. El Piwon o «jardín secreto», oculto entre sus paredes, se diseñó siguiendo el estilo del paisaje natural tradicional; durante la dinastía Joseon, era para uso exclusivo de la familia real y las concubinas del rey. El jardín incluye un estanque de lotos, pabellones, elegantes puentes de piedra, céspedes ajardinados y un enebro de 700 años de antigüedad. El pabellón albergó, en su tiempo, una biblioteca real. En ella, el rey y los cortesanos estudiaban y debatían sobre política.

Namba Parks
Osaka, Japan

Namba Parks consists of the Parks Tower office building and a 120-unit shopping mall. Completed in 2003, this urban oasis was developed by Jon Jerde on the site of the former Osaka Baseball Stadium. The most distinguishing feature of Namba Parks is undisputedly the rooftop park that connects to the street and ascends eight levels, inviting visitors into the groves of trees, lawns, water features and other natural amenities, all placed around a man-made canyon. This innovative design creates quiet pockets of green in which to dine and relax within a busy urban environment.

Namba Parks besteht aus dem Bürogebäude Parks Tower und einem Einkaufszentrum mit 120 Geschäften. Diese im Jahr 2003 fertiggestellte urbane Oase wurde von Jon Jerde auf dem Gelände des früheren Baseball-Stadions von Osaka errichtet. Das außergewöhnlichste Merkmal von Namba Parks ist zweifelsfrei der mit der Straße verbundene und acht Geschoße in die Höhe führende Dackpark, der Besucher dazu einlädt, die Haine, Wiesen, Wasserbereiche und übrigen natürlichen Annehmlichkeiten zu betreten, die eine künstliche Schlucht säumen. Diese innovative Gestaltung schafft stille und grüne Rückzugsorte inmitten einer geschäftigen städtischen Umgebung, die sich hervorragend für einen Imbiss oder zur Entspannung eignen.

Le complexe Namba Parks est formé par le gratte-ciel de bureaux Parks Tower et un centre commercial de 120 enseignes. Achevée en 2003, cette oasis urbaine a été conçue par Jon Jerde sur le site de l'ancien stade de baseball d'Osaka. Namba Parks se démarque sans conteste par sa toiture aménagée en parc qui donne accès à la rue sur un dénivelé de huit étages dans lequel bosquets d'arbres, pelouses, pièces d'eau et autres éléments naturels viennent habilement agrémenter un canyon artificiel. Cette architecture innovante permet d'agencer de véritables havres de paix naturels parfaits pour se détendre ou dîner dans un environnement urbain animé.

Los Parques Namba comprenden el edificio de oficinas Parks Tower y un centro comercial con 120 tiendas. Finalizado en 2003, este oasis urbano, obra de Jon Jerde, ocupa el emplazamiento del antiguo estadio de béisbol de Osaka. La característica más distintiva de los Parques Namba es indiscutiblemente el parque de la azotea. Comunicado con la calle, asciende ocho niveles e invita a visitar los bosquecillos de árboles, césped, instalaciones acuáticas y otras bellezas naturales, todo ello en un cañón construido por el hombre. Este innovador diseño crea unos espacios verdes apacibles, en medio de un entorno urbano concurrido, en los que cenar y relajarse.

Kenroku-en
Ishikawa, Japan

Kenroku-en is located outside the gates of Kanazawa Castle, constructed by the ruling Maeda between the sixteenth and the nineteenth centuries. Kenroku-en features ponds, streams, waterfalls, bridges, and teahouses, along with the oldest fountain in Japan. The water for the many streams and rivers of the park is diverted from a distant river by a sophisticated water system devised in 1632. The name Kenroku-en translates as 'Garden of the Six Qualities', referring to spaciousness, seclusion, artistry, maturity, abundant water and wide vistas, which, according to Chinese landscape theory, are the attributes that make the perfect garden.

Kenroku-en liegt außerhalb der Tore von Burg Kanazawa, die vom regierenden Maeda zwischen dem 16. und dem 19. Jahrhundert errichtet wurde. Neben Teichen, Bächen, Wasserfällen, Brücken und Teehäusern verfügt Kenroku-en über den ältesten Brunnen Japans. Das Nass für die zahlreichen Wasserläufe des Parks wird einem nahe gelegenen Fluss mithilfe eines 1632 errichteten ausgefeilten Bewässerungssystems entnommen. Der Name Kenroku-en lässt sich als „Garten der sechs Attribute" übersetzen und bezieht sich auf jene sechs Qualitäten, welche gemäß der chinesischen Landschafts-gestaltungstheorie einen perfekten Garten kennzeichnen, namentlich Weitläufigkeit, Abgeschiedenheit, Kunstfertigkeit, Althergebrachtes, fließendes Wasser und weiter Blick.

Kenroku-en se situe en dehors des enceintes du château de Kanazawa construit par la famille Maeda alors au pouvoir entre le seizième et le dix-neuvième siècle. Le Kenroku-en se décline autour de nombreux bassins, ruisseaux, cascades, ponts et autres maisons de thé et abrite la plus vieille fontaine du Japon. L'eau des ruisseaux et des rivières du parc est détournée d'un cours d'eau distant grâce à un système de distribution sophistiqué construit en 1632. Kenroku-en signifie « jardin des six attributs » en référence aux six qualités (espace, isolement, sens artistique, maturité, abondance d'eau et perspectives grandioses) du jardin parfait selon la tradition paysagère chinoise.

Kenroku-en se encuentra en el exterior del Castillo de Kanazawa, construido por la familia gobernante Maeda entre los siglos XVI y XIX. En Kenroku-en se pueden admirar estanques, arroyos, cascadas, puentes y casas de té, junto con la fuente más antigua de Japón. El agua para los numerosos arroyos y ríos del parque se desvió de un río lejano mediante una complejo sistema hidráulico construido en 1632. El nombre Kenroku-en significa «Jardín de las Seis Cualidades», en referencia a la espaciosidad, aislamiento, arte, madurez, agua abundante y amplias vistas que, según las teorías paisajísticas chinas, constituyen los atributos del jardín perfecto.

Completed in 1695, the Edo-period Rikugi-en is located in a quiet residential area of northern Tokyo. Yanagisawa Yoshiyasu, one of the most influential of the feudal lords, designed this garden to reflect his keen interest in poetry; the name 'Rikugi-en' means 'Garden of the Six Principles of Poetry', which refers to waka poetry. Complete with a lake, forested areas and artificial hills, the gardens became the property of the Iwasaki family, the founders of Mitsubishi, in 1878, and were donated to Tokyo City in 1938 and subsequently opened to the public.

Der im Jahr 1695 vollendete Rikugi-en oder Rikugi-Park stammt aus der Edo-Zeit und liegt in einem beschaulichen Wohnviertel im Norden Tokios. Yanagisawa Yoshiyasu, einer der einflussreichsten Lehensherren seiner Zeit, entwarf diesen Garten, um seiner großen Leidenschaft für die Dichtkunst Ausdruck zu verleihen; der Name *„Rikugi-en" bedeutet* „Garten der sechs Grundsätze der Dichtkunst" und bezieht sich auf die Waka-Dichtkunst. Die mit einem See, bewaldetem Gelände und künstlichen Hügeln ausgestatteten Gärten kamen im Jahr 1878 in den Besitz der Mitsubishi-Gründerfamilie Iwasaki, die sie 1938 der Stadt Tokio schenkte, und wurden schließlich der Öffentlichkeit zugänglich gemacht.

Rikugi-en
Tokyo, Japan

Achevé en 1695, le parc Rikugi typique de la période Edo se situe dans un quartier résidentiel tranquille au nord de Tokyo. Yanagisawa Yoshiyasu, un des seigneurs féodaux alors les plus influents, a conçu ce jardin pour refléter son grand intérêt pour la poésie; le nom « *Rikugi-en* » signifie « Jardin des six éléments de la poésie » en référence à la poésie Waka. Agrémentés d'un étang, d'espaces boisés et de collines artificielles, les jardins sont devenus la propriété de la famille Iwasaki, dont les membres ont fondé le groupe Mitsubishi, en 1878, puis furent donnés à la ville de Tokyo en 1938 et enfin ouverts par la suite au public.

Finalizado en 1695, el Rikugi-en, que data del período Edo, se encuentra en una tranquila zona residencial del norte de Tokio. Yanagisawa Yoshiyasu, uno de los señores feudales más influyentes, diseñó este jardín en el que reflejó su profundo interés por la poesía; el nombre «Rikugi-en» significa «Jardín de los Seis Principios de la Poesía» y hace referencia a la poesía waka. Completados con un lago, zonas arboladas y colinas artificiales, los jardines pasaron a ser propiedad de la familia Iwasaki, los fundadores de Mitsubishi, en 1878, que los donó a la ciudad de Tokio en 1938. Posteriormente se abrieron al público.

Melbourne's Botanic Gardens were established in 1846 by Lieutenant Governor Charles La Trobe. Over the next sixty years the swampy site near the centre of Melbourne, on the south bank of the Yarra River, was completely transformed to create these internationally renowned botanical gardens. Melbourne's mild climate allows for an eclectic mix of tropical and temperate plants, and the 38 hectares of land showcases over 10,000 individual species, including plants from the Canary Islands, New Zealand and New Caledonia. Visitors can enjoy the floral clock, the Fern Gully, Rainforest Walk and the expanses of manicured lawn.

Royal Botanic Gardens Melbourne
Melbourne, Australia

Melbournes Botanische Gärten wurden im Jahr 1846 vom Vizegouverneur Charles La Trobe begründet. Während der folgenden sechs Jahrzehnte wurde der sumpfige Standort am Südufer des Flusses Yarra und unweit der Stadtmitte Melbournes vollständig verändert, um die nunmehr international berühmten botanischen Gärten anzulegen. Das milde Klima Melbournes ermöglicht eine umfangreiche Mischung aus Pflanzen tropischer sowie gemäßigter Herkunft, und auf den 38 Hektar Land gedeihen über 10.000 individuelle Spezies, darunter Pflanzen von den Kanarischen Inseln, aus Neuseeland und Neukaledonien. Besucher können sich an einer Blumenuhr, dem Fern Gully Regenwald-Wanderweg und ausgedehnten gepflegten Rasenflächen erfreuen.

Les jardins botaniques de Melbourne ont été aménagés par le Lieutenant-Gouverneur Charles La Trobe en 1846. A l'origine marécageuse, cette zone proche du centre de Melbourne le long des berges sud de la rivière Yarra a été complètement transformée durant soixante ans pour abriter ces jardins botaniques de renommée internationale. Le climat tempéré de Melbourne est particulièrement propice à ce mélange éclectique de plantes tropicales et tempérées. Les trente-huit hectares de terrain abritent ainsi plus de 10 000 espèces différentes, parmi lesquelles des plantes des îles Canaries, de Nouvelle-Zélande et de Nouvelle-Calédonie. Les visiteurs peuvent y admirer l'horloge florale, contempler diverses espèces de fougères, déambuler dans la forêt tropicale et profiter des vastes pelouses entretenues avec soin.

El Jardín Botánico de Melbourne fue creado en 1846 por el vicegobernador Charles La Trobe. Durante los sesenta años siguientes, este pantanoso lugar próximo al centro de Melbourne, en la orilla sur del río Yarra, cambió radicalmente hasta convertirse en el actual jardín botánico de fama internacional. El suave clima de Melbourne permite una mezcla ecléctica de plantas tropicales y de clima templado. En sus 38 hectáreas de tierra se muestran más de 10.000 especies individuales, incluidas plantas de las Islas Canarias, Nueva Zelanda y Nueva Caledonia. Los visitantes pueden disfrutar del reloj floral, del Barranco de Helechos, del Paseo de la Selva Tropical y de extensas zonas de césped muy cuidado.

Chinese Garden of Friendship
New South Wales, Australia

Next to Sydney's Chinatown lies a remarkable garden that was developed to mark Australia's bicentenary in 1988, and to celebrate the friendship between Sydney and the Chinese city of Guangzhou. The walled garden was designed and built by Chinese landscape architects and gardeners, following the Taoist principles of 'yin-yang'. The garden is endowed with the traditional features of a Chinese garden: a pagoda, bamboo, weeping willows, koi carp swimming in pools, waterfalls, exotic plants, pavilions, and secluded pathways leading into brightly lit courtyards adorned with calligraphy and carvings.

In unmittelbarer Nähe zu Sydneys Chinatown befindet sich ein bemerkenswerter Garten, der zu Ehren der Zweihundertjahrfeiern Australiens im Jahr 1988 entstand, und gleichzeitig die Freundschaft zwischen Sydney und der chinesischen Stadt Guangzhou verkörpert. Der ummauerte Chinesische Garten wurde von chinesischen Landschaftsarchitekten sowie Gärtnern unter Einbeziehung des daoistischen Prinzips des „Yin und Yang" entworfen und angelegt. Der Chinesische Garten der Freundschaft verfügt über die traditionellen Merkmale eines chinesischen Gartens: eine Pagode, Bambus, Trauerweiden, ein Koi-Becken, Wasserfälle, exotische Pflanzen, Pavillons sowie abgeschiedene Pfade, die in hell erleuchteten und mittels Kalligraphie und Schnitzereien verzierten Innenhöfen münden.

Près du quartier chinois de Sydney, s'étend un jardin remarquable créé pour commémorer le bicentenaire de l'Australie en 1988 et célébrer l'amitié entre Sydney et la ville chinoise de Canton (ou Guangzhou). Ce Jardin clos chinois a été conçu et aménagé par des architectes paysagers et des jardiniers chinois selon les principes taoïstes du yin et du yang. Le jardin arbore ainsi les éléments traditionnels du jardin chinois : pagode, bambous, saules pleureurs, carpes Koi dans des bassins, cascades, plantes exotiques, pavillons et sentiers isolés donnant sur des cours lumineuses ornées de calligraphies et de statues.

Junto al Barrio Chino de Sídney se encuentra un sorprendente jardín que fue fundado para conmemorar el bicentenario de Australia en 1988 y para celebrar la amistad entre Sídney y la ciudad china de Guangzhou. El Jardín Chino amurallado fue diseñado y construido por arquitectos paisajistas y jardineros chinos, siguiendo los principios taoístas del «yin-yang». El jardín está dotado de las características tradicionales de un jardín chino: una pagoda, bambú, sauces llorones, carpas koi que nadan en estanques, cascadas, plantas exóticas, pabellones y senderos ocultos que llevan a patios luminosos adornados con caligrafías y tallas.

Butchart Gardens
British Columbia, Canada

In 1904, Robert Pim Butchart, a cement-manufacturing pioneer, came to Canada's west coast, where the rich limestone deposits allowed him to develop a quarry and build a cement plant. Five years later, his wife, Jennie, made plans to create a garden in the gigantic exhausted pit. She had tonnes of topsoil brought in and used it to line the quarry, which developed into the spectacular Sunken Garden, and over the years a Japanese garden, an Italian garden and a rose garden were added. The Buchart family still manage the gardens and the colourful array of flowers continues to draw droves of tourists every year.

Als der Zementerzeuger und Pionier Robert Pim Butchart im Jahr 1904 an die Westküste Kanadas kam, ermöglichten es ihm die reichen örtlichen Kalksteinvorkommen, einen Steinbruch sowie ein Zementwerk zu errichten. Fünf Jahre später begann seine Ehefrau Jennie damit, in der ausgebeuteten Grube einen Garten anzulegen. Sie ließ tonnenweise Mutterboden heranschaffen, mit dem sie den Steinbruch säumte, woraus schließlich der spektakuläre „Versunkene Garten" entstand; mit der Zeit sollten noch ein japanischer, ein italienischer sowie ein Rosengarten folgen. Die Gärten werden nach wie vor von der Familie Butchart betreut und die farbenfrohen Flore ziehen Jahr für Jahr Touristen in Scharen an.

En 1904, Robert Pim Butchart, pionnier de la fabrication du ciment, a débarqué sur la côte occidentale du Canada où les riches dépôts calcaires lui permirent de développer une carrière et de construire une cimenterie. Cinq ans plus tard, une fois la carrière béante épuisée, son épouse, Jennie, dessina des plans pour y aménager un jardin. Elle fit tapisser la carrière de terreau afin de créer le spectaculaire Jardin englouti (*Sunken Garden*), complété par la suite par un jardin japonais, un jardin italien et une roseraie. La famille Butchart a toujours en gestion les jardins dont les parterres de fleurs multicolores continuent d'attirer une foule de touristes chaque année.

En 1904, Robert Pim Butchart, un fabricante de cemento pionero, llegó a la costa occidental de Canadá, donde los ricos depósitos de piedra caliza le permitieron abrir una cantera y construir una fábrica de cemento. Cinco años después, su esposa, Jennie, decidió crear un jardín en la gigantesca mina agotada. Mandó traer toneladas de tierra y la utilizó para tapizar la cantera, lo que originó el espectacular Jardín Hundido. A lo largo de los años, se añadió un jardín japonés, un jardín italiano y una rosaleda. La familia Butchart sigue administrando los jardines y los coloridos parterres continúan atrayendo a infinidad de turistas todos los años.

The Desert Botanical Garden was founded in Papago Park in the northern part of the Sonora Desert by the Arizona Cactus and Native Flora Society in 1939. The aim of the garden is to research and conserve the range of plants that are found in the world's arid areas; it hosts a vast collection of agave and cactus plants, along with 139 rare and endangered plant species from around the world. Set against the dramatic backdrop of the surrounding mountains, the winding trails and oddly shaped cacti make the gardens an inspiring and educational visit.

Desert Botanical Garden
Arizona, USA

Der Desert Botanical Garden wurde im Jahr 1939 von der Arizona Cactus and Native Flora Society im Papago Park in der nördlichen Sonora-Wüste ins Leben gerufen. Das Ziel des Gartens ist die Erforschung und Erhaltung all jener Pflanzen, welche weltweit in Trockengebieten vorkommen; neben 139 seltenen und bedrohten Pflanzenarten aus allen Teilen der Erde beherbergt dieser botanische Wüstengarten eine umfangreiche Sammlung an Agave- und Kaktuspflanzen. Angesichts der beeindruckenden Bergkulisse der näheren Umgebung machen die gewundenen Pfade und seltsam geformten Kakteen jeden Gartenbesuch zu einem inspirierenden und lehrreichen Aufenthalt.

Le jardin botanique du désert a été créé sur le site du parc Papago dans la partie septentrionale du désert de Sonora par l'*Arizona Cactus and Native Flora Society* en 1939. Ce jardin est dédié à la recherche et à la conservation d'un large éventail de plantes endémiques des régions arides du monde ; il abrite une vaste collection d'agaves et de cactus, ainsi que 139 espèces végétales du monde entier rares et menacées d'extinction. Avec en toile de fond les spectaculaires chaînes montagneuses alentours, ce jardin offre au détour de ses sentiers sinueux ponctués de cactus aux formes étranges une visite aussi instructive qu'agréable.

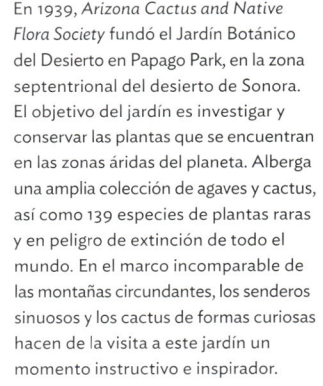

En 1939, *Arizona Cactus and Native Flora Society* fundó el Jardín Botánico del Desierto en Papago Park, en la zona septentrional del desierto de Sonora. El objetivo del jardín es investigar y conservar las plantas que se encuentran en las zonas áridas del planeta. Alberga una amplia colección de agaves y cactus, así como 139 especies de plantas raras y en peligro de extinción de todo el mundo. En el marco incomparable de las montañas circundantes, los senderos sinuosos y los cactus de formas curiosas hacen de la visita a este jardín un momento instructivo e inspirador.

Las Pozas
San Luis Potosí, Mexico

In 1949, Edward James, poet and patron to artists such as Salvador Dalí and René Magritte, began working on these tropical gardens in the Mexican jungle, aided by his friend Plutarco Gastélum. Las Pozas ('the Pools', referring to a group of small lakes in the area) hides a selection of huge and surreal sculptures, some over thirty metres tall. Winding staircases, labyrinthine paths and giant architectural follies bear the traces of James's fantastical vision of Eden. Ivan Hicks continued to work on the garden after the death its founder.

Im Jahr 1949 begann Edward James, seines Zeichens Dichter und Mäzen so berühmter Künstler wie Salvador Dalí und René Magritte, unterstützt von seinem Freund Plutarco Gastélum, mit der Arbeit an diesen tropischen Gärten im mexikanischen Dschungel. Las Pozas (die Pfützen, in Anspielung auf einige Wasserlachen in der Gegend) birgt eine Ansammlung riesenhafter und surrealer Skultpuren, von denen einige eine Höhe von über 30 Metern erreichen. Wendeltreppen, verschlungene Irrpfade und gigantische architektonische Verrücktheiten zeugen von James' fantastischen Visionen des Gartens Eden. Nach dem Tod seines Gründers setzte Ivan Hicks die Arbeiten an diesem Garten fort.

En 1949, Edward James, poète et mécène d'artistes comme Salvador Dalí et René Magritte, s'attèle à un projet de jardins tropicaux dans la jungle mexicaine, avec l'aide de son ami Plutarco Gastélum. Las Pozas (« les Bassins » en français en référence à un complexe de bassins de la région) renferment toute une série de sculptures géantes et surréalistes, certaines mesurant plus de trente mètres de haut. Escaliers en colimaçon, dédales de sentiers et autres folies architecturales démesurées témoignent de l'idée fantastique que James se faisait de l'Eden. Ivan Hicks a poursuivi les travaux après le décès de son fondateur.

En 1949, Edward James, poeta y mecenas de artistas como Salvador Dalí y René Magritte, comenzó a trabajar en estos jardines tropicales de la selva mexicana, con la ayuda de su amigo Plutarco Gastélum. Las Pozas (llamadas así por un grupo de pozas de la zona) encubren una selección de inmensas esculturas surrealistas, algunas de las cuales tienen más de treinta metros de altura. Las escaleras de caracol, los senderos laberínticos y los caprichos arquitectónicos gigantes llevan la huella de la fantástica visión del Edén de James. Tras el fallecimiento del fundador, Ivan Hicks continuó trabajando en el jardín.

Minneapolis Sculpture Garden
Minnesota, USA

Located near the Walker Art Center, the Minneapolis Sculpture Garden is home to the iconic 'Spoonbridge and Cherry', designed by husband-and-wife team Claes Oldenburg and Coosje van Bruggen. Both the park and the gardens were designed by the modernist architect Edward Larrabee Barnes. The 4.5-hectare park showcases more than forty permanent sculptures made from glass, metal, stone, and concrete, dating from 1926 to 1998. Visitors to the USA's largest sculpture garden can enjoy not only the art but also the seasonal displays in the Cowles Conservatory and the Alene Grossman Memorial Arbor and Flower Garden.

Der unweit des Walker Arts Center gelegene Skulpturengarten von Minneapolis beherbergt den legendären Spoonbridge and Cherry-Brunnen, dessen Entwurf vom Künstlerehepaar Claes Oldenburg und Coosje van Bruggen stammt. Sowohl die Anlage des Parks als auch jene der Gärten wurde vom modernistischen Architekten Edward Larrabee Barnes ersonnen. Der 4,5 Hektar große Park beherbergt über 40 permanente Skulpturen aus Glas, Metall, Stein und Beton aus der Zeit zwischen 1926 und 1998. Den Besuchern des größten Skulpturengartens des Landes wird jedoch nicht nur Kunst geboten, sondern auch saisonale Flore im Cowles Conservatory-Gewächshaus sowie der Alene-Grossman-Gedenk-Lauben- und Blumengarten.

Près du *Walker Arts Center*, le Jardin de sculptures de Minneapolis abrite l'emblématique « Spoonbridge and Cherry », œuvre du couple à la ville Claes Oldenburg et Coosje van Bruggen. Le parc et le jardin sont le fruit de l'architecte moderniste Edward Larrabee Barnes. Le parc expose sur 4,5 hectares plus de quarante sculptures permanentes faites de verre, de métal, de pierre et de béton, réalisées entre 1926 et 1998. Véritable fenêtre ouverte sur l'art, le plus grand jardin de sculptures du pays propose également aux visiteurs des expositions saisonnières dans les enceintes du *Cowles Conservatory* et de l'*Alene Grossman Memorial Arbor and Flower Garden*.

Situado a proximidad del Centro de Arte Walker, el Jardín de Esculturas de Mineápolis alberga la emblemática escultura «Spoonbridge and Cherry» (puente de cuchara y cereza), diseñada por el equipo compuesto por el matrimonio Claes Oldenburg y Coosje van Bruggen. Tanto el parque como los jardines son obra del arquitecto modernista Edward Larrabee Barnes. El parque, con una extensión de 4,5 hectáreas, muestra más de cuarenta esculturas permanentes hechas de vidrio, metal, piedra y hormigón, realizadas entre los años 1926 y 1998. Los visitantes del mayor jardín de esculturas del país pueden disfrutar no solo del arte sino también de las exposiciones temporales del Conservatorio de Cowles y del Jardín de Flores y Pérgola en recuerdo de Alene Grossman.

Chicago City Hall
Illinois, USA

In 2001, the city of Chicago saw a creative opportunity to convert the top of the City Hall, an eleven-storey office building in downtown Chicago, into a 'green roof'. Its purpose was to test how the gardens would affect temperatures and improve air quality. Placed directly amid the noisy chaos of urban life, the functioning garden is the most famous in the city. Although the rooftop is not accessible to the public, it is visible from the taller buildings in the area, a fact that influenced the design enormously.

Im Jahr 2001 ergriff die Stadt Chicago die kreative Gelegenheit dazu, das Dach jenes elfstöckigen Bürogebäudes in der Chicagoer Innenstadt umzugestalten und zu begrünen, in dem das Rasthaus untergebracht ist. Das Ziel bestand darin, die Auswirkungen von Gärten auf die Temperaturen und die Luftqualität im Gebäudeinneren herauszufinden. Heute bildet der inmitten des lautstarken urbanen Durcheinanders spriesende vollwertige Garten die berühmteste Grünfläche der Stadt. Obwohl das grüne Dach öffentlich nicht zugänglich ist, lässt sich von den größeren Gebäuden in der Umgebung ein Blick darauf erhaschen, was seine Gestaltung stark beeinflusste.

En 2001, la ville de Chicago a saisi l'incroyable opportunité de transformer la toiture de l'hôtel de ville, bâtiment administratif de onze étages situé en plein centre-ville, en « toit vert » dans l'objectif d'étudier la manière dont les jardins pourraient influer sur la température et améliorer la qualité de l'air. En prise directe avec l'effervescence bruyante de la vie urbaine, ce jardin fonctionnel est le plus connu de la ville. Si les toits ne sont pas autorisés au public, on peut toutefois admirer l'ouvrage depuis les immeubles les plus hauts du quartier, une configuration qui a énormément joué dans la conception de cet espace.

Chicago City Hall, Illinois, USA

En 2001, la ciudad de Chicago tuvo la oportunidad de convertir el tejado del City Hall, el edificio de oficinas de once plantas del ayuntamiento en pleno centro de Chicago, en un «techo verde». Su finalidad era comprobar en qué medida los jardines afectarían a la temperatura y mejorarían la calidad del aire. Situado en pleno caos de la bulliciosa vida urbana, este activo jardín es el más famoso de la ciudad. Aunque el techo no es accesible al público, es visible desde los edificios más altos de la zona, lo que influyó sobremanera en el diseño.

Museo Subacuático de Arte
Cancún, Mexico

In 2009, a monumental underwater museum was created in the waters surrounding Cancún, Isla Mujeres and Punta Nizuc, consisting of over 450 permanent life-size sculptures. The museum forms a complex reef structure for marine life to colonise, inhabit and increase biomass. Each of the sculptures is made from specialised materials used to promote coral life. The museum is divided into two galleries called Salon Manchones and Salon Nizuc. The first is eight metres deep and suitable for both divers and snorkellers, and the second is four metres deep and only suitable for snorkelling visitors.

Im Jahr 2009 wurde in den Gewässern rund um die mexikanischen Orte Cancún, Isla Mujeres und Punta Nizuc ein monumentales Unterwassermuseum errichtet, in dem über 450 lebensgroße Skulpturen dauerhaft ausgestellt werden. Das Museum bildet eine komplexe Riffstruktur, die von Meereslebewesen kolonisiert, bewohnt und mit Biomasse angereichert wird. Jede einzelne der Skulpturen besteht aus ganz besonderen Baustoffen, um die Besiedelung durch Korallen zu erleichtern. Das Museum besteht aus zwei Galerien namens Salon Manchones und Salon Nizuc. Die erste ist acht Meter tief und eignet sich sowohl für Taucher als auch für Schnorchler; die zweite ist vier Meter tief und steht ausschließlich schnorchelnden Besuchern offen.

En 2009, un monumental musée sous-marin a été créé dans les fonds marins qui bordent Cancún, les Isla Mujeres et Punta Nizuc, comprenant 450 sculptures grandeur nature permanentes. Le musée forme une structure complexe de récifs colonisés et habités par la vie marine destinés à accroître la biomasse. Chacune de ces sculptures a été fabriquée dans un matériel spécial utilisé pour promouvoir la vie corallienne. Le musée se divise en deux galeries appelées Salon Manchones et Salon Nizuc. Si la première avec ses huit mètres de profondeur convient à la fois aux plongeurs en eau profonde ou peu profonde, la seconde, qui est profonde de quatre mètres, ne satisfera que les randonneurs sous-marins équipés de tuba.

Museo Subacuático de Arte, Cancún, Mexico

En 2009, se creó un monumental museo subacuático en las aguas que rodean Cancún, Isla Mujeres y Punta Nizuc, con más de 450 esculturas permanentes de tamaño natural. El museo forma una compleja estructura de arrecifes para que la vida marina colonice, viva e incremente la biomasa. Cada una de las esculturas está hecha de materiales especiales utilizados para fomentar la vida de los corales. El museo está dividido en dos galerías llamadas Salón Manchones y Salón Nizuc. La primera tiene ocho metros de profundidad y apta tanto para buceadores como para aficionados al *snorkel*, y la segunda es de cuatro metros de profundidad y es apta solo para los que practican el *snorkel*.

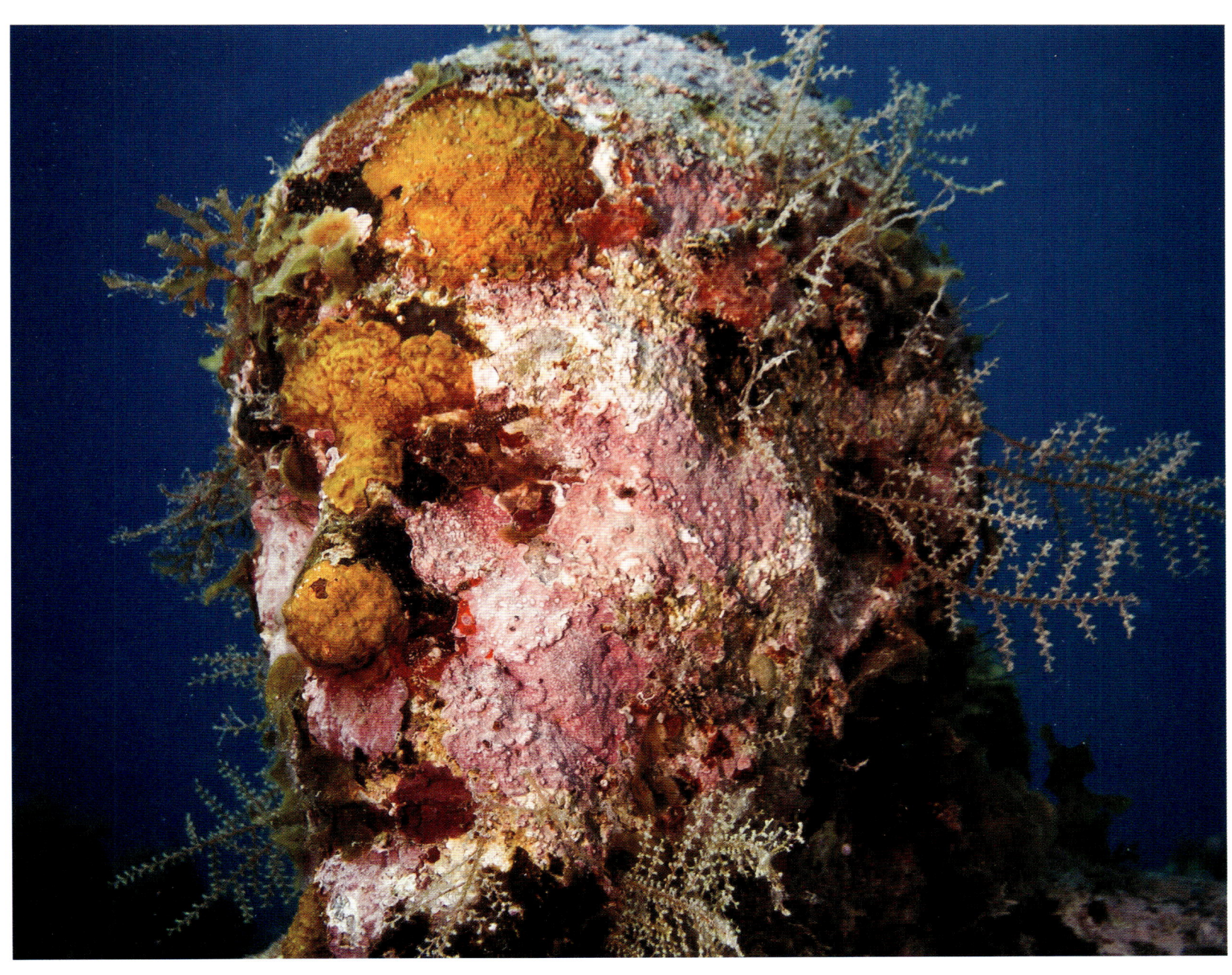

Central Park
New York, USA

Created by landscape designer Frederick Law Olmsted and architect Calvert Vaux, Central Park is perhaps the most iconic park in the world. Set on more than 300 hectares – covering over 6 per cent of the island of Manhattan – the English-style park has vast areas of open lawn, lakes, ponds, shrubberies and green avenues, providing the bustling city with an expansive natural green haven. Central Park opened to the public in 1859 and has been enormously popular with tourists, and New York joggers and skateboarders ever since.

Der vom Landschaftsarchitekten
Frederick Law Olmsted und vom
Architekten Calvert Vaux geschaffene
Central Park ist womöglich der
legendärste Park der Welt. Mit seinen
über 300 Hektar erstreckt er sich
über mehr als sechs Prozent der
Inselfläche Manhattens. Als Park im
englischen Stil bietet er ausgedehnte
offene Rasenflächen, Seen, Teiche,
Gestrüpp sowie grüne Alleen, und
dient der geschäftigen Stadt als
weitläufige, naturbelassene und grüne
Inel der Stille. Der Central Park wurde
im Jahr 1859 für die Öffentlichkeit
zugänglich gemacht und erfreut sich
seitdem bei Touristen, New Yorker
Laufbegeisterten und Skateboardern
ungebrochener Beliebtheit.

Créé par le paysagiste Frederick Law Olmsted et l'architecte Calvert Vaux, Central Park est sans doute le parc le plus emblématique du monde. Aménagé sur plus de 300 hectares répartis sur plus de 6 pour cent de l'île de Manhattan, ce parc à l'anglaise s'étend sur de vastes pelouses ouvertes agrémentées d'étangs, de ponts, d'arbustes et de pistes vertes pour offrir à l'effervescence de la ville un important havre naturel de verdure. Inauguré en 1859, Central Park reste depuis très prisé des touristes, des joggeurs et autres skateboardeurs new-yorkais.

Creado por el paisajista Frederick Law Olmsted y el arquitecto Calvert Vaux, Central Park es quizá el parque más emblemático del mundo. Este parque de estilo inglés, que se extiende a lo largo de más de 300 hectáreas (cubre más del seis por ciento de la isla de Manhattan), proporciona amplias zonas de césped, lagos, estanques, arbustos y paseos verdes, que ofrecen a la bulliciosa ciudad un gran pulmón verde natural. Tras su apertura al público en 1859, Central Park ha logrado desde entonces una gran popularidad entre turistas, corredores y patinadores de Nueva York.

Built on a railway elevated above Manhattan's West Side, the High Line is an aerial greenway serving as a public park running from Gansevoort Street in the Meatpacking District to West 34th Street, between 10th and 11th Avenues. A similar project in Paris, the 4.8-kilometre Promenade plantée, was the inspiration. It has been hailed as one of the most innovative and inviting public spaces in New York City. Walking on the High Line is unlike any other urban experience, as you are at once removed from the cityscape and yet connected to it.

High Line
New York, USA

Die im Westen Manhattens auf einer ehemaligen Hochbahntrasse errichtete High Line ist ein luftiger Grünzug, der als öffentlicher Park fungiert und von der Gansevoort Street im Meatpacking District bis zur West 34th Street, zwischen 10th und 11th Avenue verläuft. Die High Line inspiriert sich an einem ähnlichen Projekt aus Paris, der 4,8 Kilometer langen „Promenade plantée". Dieses Projekt wurde als einer der innovativsten und einladensten öffentlichen Plätze der Stadt New York gefeiert. Aufgrund der gleichzeitigen Entrücktheit und Allgegenwart der Stadtviertel lässt sich ein Spaziergang entlang der High Line mit keiner anderen städtischen Erfahrung vergleichen.

Construite sur une portion désaffectée des voies ferrées aériennes du West Side à Manhattan, la High Line désigne à la fois une voie verte suspendue et un parc public reliant Gansevoort Street dans le Meatpacking District à la 34ème rue West, entre la 10ème et la 11ème Avenues. La High Line s'est inspirée d'un projet similaire à Paris, la Promenade plantée de 4,8 kilomètres de long. Elle a été saluée comme étant l'un des espaces publics newyorkais les plus novateurs et conviviaux qui soit. La High Line offre une expérience urbaine incomparable où le temps d'une promenade, vous êtes déconnecté de la ville sans pour autant la quitter physiquement.

Construida sobre una vía de tren elevada por encima del West Side de Manhattan, la High Line es un camino verde aéreo que funciona como parque público desde la calle Gansevoort, en el distrito de Meatpacking, hasta la calle 34 Oeste, entre la Décima y la Novena Avenidas. Un proyecto similar en París, la *Promenade Plantée* de 4,8 km, sirvió de inspiración. Ha sido aclamado como uno de los espacios públicos más innovadores y atractivos de la ciudad de Nueva York. Pasear por la High Line no es equiparable a ninguna otra experiencia urbana, ya que uno se encuentra de repente aislado del paisaje urbano pero sigue conectado a él.

Founded in 1931 by mayor Camillien
Houde after years of campaigning
by Brother Marie-Victorin, the Jardin
botanique de Montréal is set centrally
on 75 hectares. The gardens are
thriving and diverse, and present a
remarkably impressive array of plants.
Highlights include a Japanese garden,
a Chinese garden, a tree house,
an insectarium, interactive displays
and a First Nations garden. It was
designated a National Historic Site of
Canada in 2008, and it is considered to
be one of the most important botanical
gardens in the world due to the extent
of its collections and facilities.

Der 1931 von Bürgermeister Camillien
Houde auf langjähriges Betreiben
des Ordensbruders Marie-Victorin
gegründete botanische Garten von
Montreal erstreckt sich im Herzen
der Stadt auf einer Fläche von über 75
Hektar. Die Gärten zeichnen sich durch
üppigen und vielfältigen Bewuchs sowie
eine bemerkenswerte Pflanzenvielfalt
aus. Zu den Sehenswürdigkeiten zählen
ein japanischer sowie ein chinesischer
Garten, ein Baumhaus, ein Insektarium,
interaktive Anzeigen und ein den Ersten
Nationen gewidmeter Garten. Im Jahr
2008 wurde der botanische Garten als
Denkmal von historischer Bedeutung
in die Liste der National Historic Sites
of Canada aufgenommen. Aufgrund
seiner umfangreichen Sammlungen und
Anlagen gilt er als einer der bedeutensten
botanischen Gärten der Welt.

Créé en 1931 par le maire Camillien Houde après des années de campagne menée par le frère Marie-Victorin, le Jardin botanique de Montréal prend place en plein cœur de la ville sur soixante-quinze hectares. Florissants et diversifiés, ces jardins abritent une collection de plantes particulièrement impressionnante. Le jardin japonais, le jardin de Chine, la maison de l'arbre, l'insectarium, les expositions interactives, sans oublier le jardin des premières nations en forment les principaux points marquants. Reconnu lieu historique national du Canada en 2008, le jardin botanique est considéré comme l'un des plus importants au monde en raison de l'étendue de ses collections et de ses installations.

Fundado en 1931 por el alcalde Camillien Houde, tras años de campañas llevadas a cabo por el hermano Marie-Victorin, el Jardín Botánico de Montreal se encuentra en medio de 75 hectáreas. Los jardines, florecientes y variados, presentan una diversidad de plantas realmente impresionante. Entre los elementos más destacados se encuentran un jardín japonés, un jardín chino, una casa en un árbol, un insectario, exposiciones interactivas y un jardín de las primeras naciones. Fue declarado Sitio Histórico Nacional de Canadá en 2008 y está considerado como uno de los jardines botánicos más importantes del mundo debido a la gran extensión de sus colecciones e instalaciones.

Gilberto Strunk Residence
Petropolis, Brazil

Designed by the famed Brazilian landscape architect and artist Roberto Burle Marx, this house was originally named the Edmundo Cavanellas Residence. The garden, which occupies a large valley, provides the setting for an Oscar Niemeyer-designed modernist house. The garden is an example of the avant-garde style of Burle Marx's work, which challenged the established European aesthetic of the time. The most remarkable feature is the chequerboard pattern made up of differing shades of Stenotaphrum. In front of the house, curved forms lie before the large pond, leading the eye to the spectacular views of the surrounding landscape.

Dessinée par le célèbre architecte paysager et artiste brésilien Roberto Burle Marx, cette résidence portait à l'origine le nom d'Edmundo Cavanellas. Le jardin, encaissé dans une immense vallée, sert de cadre à une maison moderne conçue par Oscar Niemeyer. Ce jardin illustre à merveille le style avant-gardiste du travail de Burle Marx, qui a complètement bousculé les codes de l'esthétique européenne en vogue à l'époque. Le jardin se distingue notamment par son motif en damier obtenu grâce à l'agencement de différentes déclinaisons de *Stenotaphrum*. Devant la maison s'étirent des parterres dont les formes incurvées donnent sur un grand bassin et invitent à admirer l'incroyable paysage naturel environnant.

Diseñada por el célebre arquitecto paisajista y artista brasileño Roberto Burle Marx, esta residencia se llamaba originalmente Residencia Edmundo Cavanellas. El jardín, que ocupa un amplio valle, proporciona el marco a una casa modernista diseñada por Oscar Niemeyer. Este jardín constituye todo un ejemplo del estilo vanguardista característico de la obra de Burle Marx, que desafió la estética oficial europea de su tiempo. El rasgo más destacable es su diseño ajedrezado, formado por distintos tonos de *Stenotaphrum*. Frente a la casa, unas formas curvas, ante el amplio estanque, dirigen la mirada a las vistas espectaculares del paisaje circundante.

Die vom berühmten brasilianischen Landschaftsarchitekten und Künstler Roberto Burle Marx gestaltete Residenz trug ursprünglich den Namen Casa Edmundo Cavanellas. Der Garten, der sich über ein breites Tal erstreckt, beherbergt ein von Oscar Niemeyer entworfenes modernistisches Gebäude und steht beispielhaft für den avantgardistischen Stil der Werke Burle Marx', der die etablierte europäische Ästhetik seiner Zeit infrage stellte. Das auffälligste Merkmal bildet das aus farblich abgestuften *Stenotaphrum* bestehende Schachbrettmuster. Vor dem Haus erstrecken sich geschwungene Formen zu allen Seiten des großen Teichs und lenken den Blick zu den spektakulären Panoramen der umliegenden Landschaften.

Jardin Majorelle
Marrakech, Morroco

Jardin Majorelle, Marrakech, Morocco

Le Jardin Majorelle is surely one of the world's most visually engaging gardens, filled as it is with bold, optimistic shades of blue, green and yellow. It was created by the French painter and passionate amateur botanist Jacques Majorelle. In 1980, Yves Saint Laurent bought the garden to stop it from becoming a hotel complex, and he began to restore it in keeping with the vision of Majorelle. The garden radiates with multicoloured bougainvillea, rows of bright orange nasturtiums, and pink geraniums. There are paths in shades of pastel pink, lemon and apple green, and more than fifteen different species of birds have made the garden their home.

Der mit kühnen, optimistischen Blau-, Grün- und Gelbnuancen angereicherte Jardin Majorelle zählt zweifelsfrei zu den optisch ansprechendsten Gärten der Welt. Er wurde vom französischen Maler und leidenschaftlichen Amateurbotanisten Jacques Majorelle ins Leben gerufen. Im Jahr 1980 kaufte Yves Saint Laurent den Garten, um ihn der Vision Majorelles gemäß zu restaurieren, und dessen Umwandlung in einen Hotelkomplex zu verhindern. Bunte Bougainvillea, Reihen leuchtend oranger Brunnenkressen und rosarote Pelargonien bringen den Garten regelrecht zum Strahlen. Pfade in den Schattierungen Pastellrosa, Zitrone und Apfelgrün führen durch diesen Garten, den sich über fünfzehn verschiedene Vogelarten zur Heimstätte erkoren haben.

Le Jardin Majorelle est certainement l'un des jardins à offrir l'une des visions les plus chatoyantes qui soit au monde, oscillant entre d'incroyables nuances de bleu vif revigorant (bleu Majorelle), de vert et de jaune. Créé par le peintre et grand amateur botaniste français, Jacques Majorelle, le jardin fut racheté en 1980 par Yves Saint Laurent qui stoppa le projet destiné à en faire un complexe hôtelier pour débuter une restauration fidèle à la vision initiale de Majorelle. Le jardin rayonne littéralement dans un panaché de bougainvilliers multicolores, de rangées de capucines orange vif et de géraniums roses. Les sentiers, entre ombre et lumière, se parent tour à tour de rose pastel, de jaune et de vert pomme et offrent un refuge végétal à plus de quinze espèces d'oiseaux différents.

Jardín Majorelle, Marrakech, Morroco

El Jardín Majorelle es sin duda uno de los jardines más atractivos del mundo desde un punto de vista visual, gracias a sus atrevidos y optimistas tonos azules, verdes y amarillos. Fue creado por el pintor francés Jacques Majorelle, que era además un gran aficionado a la botánica. En 1980, Yves Saint Laurent adquirió el jardín para impedir que se convirtiera en un complejo hotelero y comenzó a restaurarlo respetando la visión de Majorelle. El jardín rebosa de buganvillas multicolores, filas de capuchinas de color naranja brillante y geranios rosas. Lo recorren sendas en tonos rosa pastel, limón y verde manzana, y más de quince especies de aves distintas anidan en el jardín.

Established in 1795 by the Dublin Society, Dublin's botanic gardens, situated on the River Tolka, are best known for the beauty of the nineteenth-century greenhouses, including the Great Palm House and the Turner Curvilinear Range. The beauty of these gardens is not limited to the greenhouses, however, owing to its elegant rockeries, rose garden, pond and a Chinese plant collection. Conversation plays an important role in the life of these botanic gardens, which preserve a number of species that are now extinct in the wild, and in all they are home to over 20,000 plants, both native and exotic.

Die im Jahr 1795 von der Dublin Society am Fluss Tolka angelegten botanischen Gärten Dublins sind in erster Linie für die Schönheit der aus dem 19. Jahrhundert stammenden Gewächshäuser bekannt, darunter das Große Palmenhaus und das Turner Curvilinear Range. Die Anmut dieser Gärten beschränkt sich jedoch keineswegs auf die Treibhäuser, sondern speist sich weiters aus den eleganten Stein- und Rosengärten, dem Teich sowie der Sammlung chinesischer Pflanzen. Das Erhalten bedrohter Arten wird von den botanischen Gärten groß geschrieben, weshalb sie neben über 20.000 einheimischen wie exotischen Pflanzen, die allesamt hier ein Zuhause gefunden haben, eine ganze Reihe an Spezies bewahren, die in freier Natur bereits ausgestorben sind.

Aménagés en 1975 par la *Dublin Society*, au bord de la rivière Tolka, les jardins botaniques de Dublin sont renommés pour la beauté de leurs serres du dix-neuvième siècle dont la serre aux palmiers (*Great Palm House*) et le bâtiment curviligne (*Turner Curvilinear Range*). La beauté de ces jardins ne saurait toutefois se limiter aux serres: un élégant jardin de rocaille, une roseraie, un étang et une collection de plantes chinoises finissent de parfaire le tableau. Les jardins botaniques mettent également à l'honneur la conservation puisqu'ils abritent un certain nombre d'espèces aujourd'hui éteintes à l'état sauvage. Les jardins recensent en tout plus de 20 000 plantes indigènes comme exotiques.

Fundado en 1795 por la Dublin Society, el jardín botánico de Dublín, situado junto al río Tolka, es famoso por la belleza de sus invernaderos decimonónicos, incluidos la Great Palm House y el Turner Curvilinear Range. No obstante, la belleza de este jardín no se limita a los invernaderos, destacan igualmente las elegantes rocallas, la rosaleda, el estanque y una colección de plantas chinas. La conservación desempeña una importante función en la vida del jardín botánico, que preserva algunas especies actualmente extinguidas en su hábitat natural; alberga más de 20.000 plantas, tanto nativas como locales.

Powerscourt
Wicklow, Ireland

The gardens at Powerscourt are famed for their spectacular setting and the panoramic views they offer of the Great Sugar Loaf Mountain. Despite being laid out over two main periods, the gardens adorning the Palladian mansion house are largely the design of the London architect Daniel Robertson, who was one of the leading proponents of Italianate garden design. Set on almost 20 hectares, visitors today enjoy its Triton pool and fountain, the Italian and Japanese gardens, statues and ornamental lakes, rambling walks, tree-lined avenues, cascades, grottos and a very unusual pet cemetery.

Die Gärten von Powerscourt verdanken ihre Berühmtheit der spektakulären Landschaftskulisse und den atemberaubenden Aussichten auf den Höhenkamm des Great Sugar Loaf (Großer Zuckerhut). Obwohl sie zu zwei verschiedenen Hauptperioden angelegt wurden, spiegeln die Gärten, die das palladianische Herrenhaus zieren, weitestgehend die Anlage durch den Londoner Architekten Daniel Robertson wider, der als einer der Hauptvertreter der italienischen Gartengestaltung galt. Besucher der beinahe 20 Hektar großen Anlage erfreuen sich heutzutage vor allem am Tritonsee und -brunnen, an den italienischen und japanischen Garten, sowie an Statuen und Zierteichen, ausgedehnten Flanierwegen, baumgesäumten Alleen, Wasserfällen, Grotten und an einem mehr als ungewöhnlichen Haustierfriedhof.

Les jardins de la propriété Powerscourt sont renommés pour leur cadre incroyable et la vue panoramique qu'ils offrent de la montagne Great Sugar Loaf. Bien qu'ils aient été aménagés sur deux périodes distinctes, les jardins qui ornent une demeure de style palladien ont été pour l'essentiel conçus par l'architecte londonien Daniel Robertson, fervent partisan des jardins à l'italienne. Sur près de 20 hectares, les visiteurs peuvent aujourd'hui y admirer le bassin et la fontaine de Triton, des jardins italiens et japonais, des statues et des pièces d'eau, emprunter les sentiers de randonnée et les chemins bordés d'arbres, explorer les cascades, les grottes et un cimetière d'animaux peu commun.

Los Jardines de Powerscourt son famosos por el espectacular entorno en el que se encuentran y por las vistas panorámicas que ofrecen de la montaña Great Sugar Loaf. A pesar de haberse creado a lo largo de dos épocas principales, los jardines que adornan la mansión, de estilo palladiano, son mayoritariamente obra del arquitecto londinense Daniel Robertson, uno de los máximos defensores del diseño de jardines a la italiana. Con una extensión de casi 20 hectáreas, a este jardín acuden los visitantes actuales para disfrutar de la charca y la fuente de Tritón, los jardines italiano y japonés, las estatuas y los lagos ornamentales, los intrincados senderos, los paseos arbolados, las cascadas, las grutas y un insólito cementerio de mascotas.

The Lost Gardens of Heligan
Cornwall, England

In 1992, a group of volunteers set about revealing these gardens from under a thick blanket of decayed vegetation, where they had been hiding since the First World War. Situated on the estate on which the Cornish Tremayne family were resident for over 400 years, the Lost Gardens of Heligan offer the visitor over 80 hectares to explore. It was created in the nineteenth-century gardenesque style, with distinct areas offering different gardens types, including the romantic Victorian Productive Gardens, the Italian Gardens, and an exotic outdoor jungle.

Im Jahr 1992 begann eine Gruppe
Freiwilliger damit, diese Gärten von der
sie erstickenden Schicht verrottender
Vegetation zu befreien, unter der sie
seit dem Ersten Weltkrieg verborgen
lagen. Die *Verlorenen Gärten von Heligan*
befinden sich auf jenem Anwesen,
das der kornischen Familie Tremayne
über 400 Jahre lang als Residenz diente,
und bieten Besuchern die Möglichkeit,
mehr als 80 Hektar Gartenlandschaft
zu entdecken. Sie wurden im 19.
Jahrhundert im Gardenesque-Stil
angelegt, bei dem einzelne Bereiche
unterschiedlichen Gartentypen
gewidmet sind, und locken mit
einem romantischen viktorianischen
Nutzgarten, italienischen Gärten und
einem exotischen Freilanddschungel.

En 1992, un grupo de voluntarios descubrieron estos jardines debajo de una gruesa capa de vegetación descompuesta, bajo la que había permanecido ocultos desde la Primera Guerra Mundial. Situados en la propiedad en la que residió la familia Tremayne de Cornualles durante más de 400 años, los Jardines Perdidos de Heligan ofrecen al visitante más de ochenta hectáreas para explorar. Se crearon en el estilo Gardenesque del siglo XIX, con áreas diferenciadas que ofrecen distintos tipos de jardines, incluidos jardines productivos románticos victorianos, jardines italianos y una jungla exótica al aire libre.

En 1992, un groupe de bénévoles s'est attelé à révéler ces jardins jusqu'alors enfouis sous une épaisse couche de végétation en décomposition depuis la Première Guerre mondiale. Situés dans la propriété où a résidé la famille cornouaillaise Tremayne pendant plus de 400 ans, les Jardins perdus de Heligan offrent au visiteur plus de quatre-vingt hectares à explorer. Ils ont été aménagés dans le style dit « Gardenesque » du dix-neuvième siècle et se divise en espaces distincts aménagés en différents types de jardins, dont les jardins romantiques victoriens, les jardins à l'italienne et une jungle luxuriante naturelle.

Eden Project
Cornwall, England

After having restored The Lost Gardens of Heligan, Tim Smit turned his attention to the design of these epic and awe-inspiring biodomes, on the site of a reclaimed Kaolinite pit, to showcase plants collected from all around the world. A tropical environment is created in one biosphere and a warm, temperate climate is created in the other, providing diverse growing conditions for over one thousand plant species, and streams and waterfalls. The Eden Project has an educational focus, and draws visitors' attention to the delicate balance of living things in our environment.

Nach der Wiederherstellung der Lost Gardens of Heligan wandte sich Tim Smit der Gestaltung dieser epischen und ehrfurchtgebietenden Biodome zu, um auf dem Gelände einer renaturierten Kaolinit-Grube Pflanzen aus allen Ecken und Enden der Erde der Öffentlichkeit zu präsentieren. Eine der Biosphären dient beispielsweise der Erschaffung einer tropischen Umgebung, während in einer anderen ein warmes, gemäßigtes Klima vorherrscht, um so unterschiedlichste Wachstumsbedingungen für über tausend Pflanzenarten sowie Wasserläufe und Wasserfälle bereitzustellen. Das Eden-Projekt zielt auf die Vermittlung von Wissen ab und will die Aufmerksamkeit der Besucher auf das delikate Gleichgewicht zwischen Lebewesen in unserer Umgebung lenken.

Après avoir restauré les Jardins perdus de Heligan (Lost Gardens of Heligan), Tim Smit s'est attelé à la conception de ces dômes géodésiques aussi grandioses que surréalistes sur le site d'une ancienne carrière de kaolin recyclée dans le but d'y exposer des plantes issues du monde entier. Une des biosphères reproduit un climat tropical, alors que l'autre recréé un milieu chaud et tempéré offrant ainsi diverses conditions de développement au millier d'espèces végétales plantées parmi les ruisseaux et chutes d'eau du complexe. A vocation pédagogique, l'Eden Project attire l'attention des visiteurs sur le fragile équilibre entre les espèces vivant dans notre environnement.

Tras haber restaurado los Jardines Perdidos de Heligan, Tim Smit volcó su atención en el diseño de estos geniales e impresionantes biodomos, en el emplazamiento de una mina de caolinita recuperada, para exhibir plantas recogidas en todas las partes del mundo. Se ha creado un entorno tropical en una biosfera y, en la otra, un clima templado y cálido, lo que proporciona unas condiciones de crecimiento distintas para más de un millar de especies vegetales; a todo ello, se han sumado arroyos y cascadas. El Proyecto Edén tiene una finalidad educativa y atrae la atención de los visitantes hacia el delicado equilibrio de los seres vivos en el medio ambiente.

Bodnant Garden
Conwy, Wales

Amongst the many virtues of Bodnant Garden, situated above the River Conwy, the epic view over the eastern edge of the Carneddau mountain range must be its most alluring. Henry Ponchin bought the estate in 1874, and several generations of his family have since worked to bring the garden to its present-day beauty. It was presented to the National Trust in 1949. The initial design was the work of Edward Milner, who laid out expansive lawns and conceived the famous tunnel, from which hang luscious yellow laburnum. Other highlights include the grand formal terraces, the Chinese rhododendrons, and the Dell: a deep valley with streams, and towering trees.

Von den zahlreichen Vorzügen des über dem Fluss Conwy gelegenen Bodnant Garden zählt der märchenhafte Blick über die östlichen Ausläufer der Carneddau-Gebirgskette wohl zu den reizvollsten. Seit Henry Ponchin das Anwesen im Jahr 1874 erwarb, arbeiteten mehrere Generationen seiner Familie emsig daran, dem Garten seine heutige Schönheit zu verleihen. Im Jahr 1949 wurde es der Kultur- und Naturschutzorganisation National Trust übergeben. Die ursprüngliche Anlage stammt von Edward Milner, der weitläufige Rasenflächen anlegte und den berühmten und mit gelbem Goldregen behangenen Tunnel entwarf. Zu den übrigen Sehenswürdigkeiten gehören die großen formalen Terrassen, die chinesischen Rhododendren und das „Dell": ein tiefes, von Bächen durchzogenes und von mächtigen Bäumen bewachsenes Tal.

Parmi les nombreuses merveilles qu'offre le jardin Bodnant, qui surplombe la rivière Conwy, la vue imprenable sur le flanc oriental de la chaîne montagneuse de Carneddau est sans nul doute la plus saisissante. Le domaine a été acquis par Henry Ponchin en 1874. Depuis, plusieurs générations de la même famille ont œuvré à préserver le jardin dans toute sa splendeur actuelle. Le jardin a été présenté au *National Trust* (association à but non lucratif britannique dédiée à la conservation et à la mise en valeur des monuments et des sites d'intérêt collectif) en 1949. Le jardin doit sa conception originale aux travaux d'Edward Milner, qui a aménagé de vastes pelouses et dessiné le célèbre tunnel dont l'arc voûté est formé par de somptueux cytises suspendus dans les tons jaunes. Le jardin se distingue également par ses grandes terrasses solennelles, ses rhododendrons de Chine et le *Dell* : un profond vallon parcouru de ruisseaux et de hautes futaies.

Entre las muchas virtudes del Jardín Bodnant, que domina el río Conwy, destacan ante todo las soberbias vistas que se disfrutan del lado oriental de la cordillera de Carneddau. Tras la adquisición de esta propiedad por parte de Henry Ponchin en 1874, varias generaciones de la familia se han dedicado desde entonces a embellecer el jardín hasta llevarlo a su actual esplendor. En 1949 pasó a formar parte del National Trust (fundación para la conservación del patrimonio británico). El diseño inicial fue obra de Edward Milner, que implantó amplias zonas de césped y diseñó el famoso túnel del que cuelgan exquisitos citisos amarillos. Entre sus elementos más emblemáticos sobresalen las magníficas terrazas de diseño formal, los rododendros chinos y la Hondonada: un hondo valle con arroyos y árboles imponentes.

Drummond Castle Gardens
Perthshire, Scotland

Built by John, 1ˢᵗ Lord Drummond, this composite garden has evolved over fifty years, and bears the mark of many generations of the Drummond family and characteristics of different time periods. The dominant feature of the parterre design is a Saint Andrew's Cross with a seventeenth-century sundial at its centre. A long north–south axis runs through the garden, down a flight of steps, through a classical archway and into dense woodland, before rising to the top of the opposing hillside. This idea of drawing the countryside into the garden is essentially French, however Drummond is also rooted firmly in the Italian style, with its urns, fountains, and statues.

Dieser von John, dem ersten Lord Drummond, errichtete Mischgarten entstand über einen Zeitraum von 500 Jahren und trägt die Handschrift zahreicher Generationen der Drummond-Familie sowie Merkmale unterschiedlichster Epochen. Das dominierende Charakteristikum der Parterre-Anlage ist das Andreaskreuz samt zentraler Sonnenuhr aus dem 17. Jahrhundert. Eine lange Nord-Süd-Achse verläuft durch den Garten und über eine Treppe, durchquert einen klassischen Bogengang sowie dichtes Gehölz und endet schließlich am gegenüberliegenden Hügelkamm. Obwohl die Idee, die Landschaft in den Garten zu holen, ursprünglich aus Frankreich stammt, finden sich im Schlossgarten von Drummond auch Zeugnisse des italienischen Stils, namentlich Urnen, Brunnen und Statuen.

Conçu par John Drummond 1er, Lord Drummond, ce jardin varié a beaucoup évolué en cinq cent ans. Fortement marqué par la signature de nombreuses générations successives de Drummond, il arbore également certaines caractéristiques propres à différentes époques. Le parterre se distingue par son aménagement en croix de Saint-André avec en son centre un cadran solaire du dix-septième siècle. Traversé dans toute sa longueur par un axe nord-sud qui prend naissance au bas d'un grand escalier, le jardin donne, après avoir passé une arche de type classique, sur une forêt dense avant de s'élever jusqu'au sommet de la colline opposée. Si l'idée de faire entrer la campagne dans le jardin est d'inspiration essentiellement française, l'aménagement du jardin avec ses urnes, ses fontaines et ses statues est profondément ancré dans la tradition italienne.

Construido por John, primer Lord Drummond, este variado jardín ha evolucionado durante más de quinientos años: lleva la huella de numerosas generaciones de la familia Drummond y las características de los distintos períodos. El rasgo predominante del diseño del parterre es una cruz de San Andrés con un reloj de sol del siglo XVII en el centro. Un largo eje norte-sur recorre todo el jardín: hacia abajo por un tramo de escaleras, a través de un arco de entrada clásico y en medio de un denso bosque, antes de finalizar subiendo a la cima de la ladera opuesta. La idea de introducir la campiña en el jardín es esencialmente francesa, no obstante, Drummond está profundamente enraizado en el estilo italiano, gracias a sus urnas, fuentes y estatuas.

Royal Botanic Gardens, Kew
London, England

Usually referred to as Kew Gardens, these extensive gardens hold the world's largest and most comprehensive collection of living plants. During the eighteenth century, Kew Palace was used as a summer residence by the British Royal Family. What started as a small 'Physick Garden' on the grounds has evolved into immense world-famous gardens, comprising a treetop walkway, magnificent glasshouses, a pagoda, an art gallery and a number of temples, aside from the dizzying array of plant collections. In 2003, it became a UNESCO World Heritage site.

Souvent appelés *Kew Gardens* (jardins de Kew), ces immenses jardins abritent la collection de plantes vivantes la plus complète et la plus importante au monde. Au dix-huitième siècle, la famille royale britannique établissait sa résidence d'été au *Kew Palace*. Le modeste « jardin de plantes médicinales » aménagé à l'origine s'est transformé depuis en un immense parc de renommée internationale, et comprend désormais une passerelle à travers la canopée d'arbres, des serres à couper le souffle, une pagode, une galerie d'art et un nombre important de temples, sans oublier un incroyable éventail de collections de plantes. Les jardins ont été inscrits au patrimoine mondial de l'UNESCO en 2003.

Die für gewöhnlich einfach als Kew Gardens bezeichneten weitläufigen königlichen botanischen Gärten beherbergen die weltweit größte und umfassendste Sammlung lebender Pflanzen. Während des 18. Jahrhunderts diente Kew Palace dem britischen Königshaus als Sommerresidenz. Was hier einst als kleiner „Physick Garden" oder Heilkräutergarten begann, entwickelte sich schließlich zu ausgedehnten Gärten von Weltruhm. Neben der atemberaubenden Pflanzensammlung verfügt diese Anlage über einen Baumkronenpfad, beeindruckende Gewächshäuser, eine Pagode, eine Kunstgalerie sowie zahlreiche Tempel. Im Jahr 2003 wurden die Gärten von Kew zum UNESCO-Weltkulturerbe erhoben.

Comúnmente conocidos como Jardines de Kew, estos amplios jardines albergan la colección más amplia y exhaustiva de plantas vivas del mundo. Durante el siglo XVIII, el Palacio de Kew se utilizó como residencia de verano de la familia real británica. Lo que comenzó siendo un pequeño «jardín de plantas medicinales» en el terreno ha evolucionado hasta convertirse en unos inmensos jardines de renombre mundial, que incluyen una pasarela colgante, unos espléndidos invernaderos, una pagoda, una galería de arte y algunos templos, además de la abrumadora diversidad de las colecciones de plantas. En 2003, fueron declarados Patrimonio de la Humanidad de la UNESCO.

Villandry, finished around 1536, is the last of the large castles to have been built on the banks of the Loire during the Renaissance. Ever since its construction, lavish gardens have embraced the building. These were victim to changes in garden aesthetic over the years, and underwent many drastic changes to bring them into line with the fashions of times. The château was bought by Dr Joachim Carvallo in 1906 and, with the help of fourteenth-century texts, he spent eighteen years restoring the elaborate gardens to their original strict geometric layout.

Beim 1536 fertiggestellten Château de Villandry handelt es sich um das letzte der während der Renaissance am Ufer der Loire errichteten Prunkschlösser. Bereits seit seiner Gründung wird dieses Gebäude von verschwenderischen Gärten umrahmt. Mit den Jahren wurden diese Grünanlagen immer wieder das Opfer einer sich verändernden Gartenästhetik, was weitreichende Umgestaltungen zur Folge hatte, um dem jeweils vorherrschenden Schönheitsempfinden der Zeit genüge zu tun. Das Schloss wurde 1906 von einem gewissen Dr. Joachim Carvallo erstanden, der 18 Jahre damit verbrachte, die aufwendigen Gärten mithilfe historischer Texte aus dem 14. Jahrhundert zu restaurieren und ihnen ihre strenge geometrische Originalgestalt zurückzugeben.

Villandry, dont les travaux furent achevés vers 1536, est le dernier château à avoir été érigé sur les berges de la Loire durant la Renaissance. Depuis le début même de sa construction, de somptueux jardins entourent l'édifice. Au gré des tendances esthétiques qui se succédèrent, ces jardins ont toutefois connu de nombreuses et impressionnantes transformations pour coller aux modes du moment. Le château fut racheté en 1906 par le Dr Joachim Carvallo qui, avec l'aide d'ouvrages du quatorzième siècle, passa dix-huit ans à restaurer ces jardins sophistiqués jusqu'à leur redonner leur forme d'origine à la géométrie si stricte.

Villandry, finalizado hacia 1536, es el último de los grandes castillos que se construyeron a orillas del Loira durante el Renacimiento. Desde su construcción, el edificio ha estado siempre rodeado por espléndidos jardines. A lo largo de los años, éstos han sido víctima de los cambios en la estética del paisajismo y han sufrido transformaciones drásticas para adaptarlos a las modas del momento. El castillo fue adquirido por el Dr. Joachim Carvallo en 1906 que, con ayuda de textos del siglo XIV, pasó dieciocho años restableciendo los elaborados jardines a su estricto diseño geométrico original.

The Château de Marqueyssac is a seventeenth-century building offering superb panoramic views of the Dordogne valley. It was built by Bertrand Vernet de Marqueyssac, Counsellor to Louis XIV. In 1861, it was inherited by Julien de Cerval, who had a passion for gardens, having spent time in Italy. He redesigned the series of terraced gardens and planted more than 150,000 boxwood trees carved into fantastical rounded shapes. Beginning in 1996, Kléber Rossillon, the new owner, restored the gardens, keeping their old character while adding some new features, including an alley of santolina and rosemary, and a cascading waterfall.

Beim Château Marqueyssac handelt es sich um ein Gebäude aus dem 17. Jahrhundert, das herrliche Panoramen über das Dordogne-Tal bietet. Es wurde von Bertrand Vernet de Marqueyssac errichtet, seines Zeichens Berater Ludwig XIV. Im Jahr 1861 ging das Anwesen in Form einer Erbschaft an Julien de Cerval, der von seinen Italienaufenthalten eine Leidenschaft für Gärten mitgebracht hatte. Er gestaltete sämtliche terrassierten Gärten um und pflanzte über 150.000 Buchsbäume, die er in fantastische runde Formen schneiden ließ. Beginnend mit 1996 setzte der neue Eigentümer Kléber Rossillon die Gärten wieder instand, wobei auf die Beibehaltung ihres ursprünglichen Charakters bei gleichzeitiger Hinzufügung einiger neuer Merkmale geachtet wurde, darunter eine Allee aus Heiligenkraut und Rosmarin sowie eine Kaskade.

Le château de Marqueyssac du dix-septième siècle offre une vue panoramique incomparable sur la vallée de Dordogne. L'édifice fut construit par Bertrand Vernet de Marqueyssac, conseiller du roi Louis XIV. En 1861, le château fut légué à Julien de Cerval, grand passionné de jardins après un séjour en Italie. Il a donc redessiné les jardins en terrasses et planté plus de 150 000 buis taillés en formes arrondies tout droit sortis d'un univers fantastique. Le nouveau propriétaire des lieux, Kléber Rossillon, a débuté la restauration des jardins en 1996 en veillant à préserver leur nature ancestrale tout en ajoutant de nouveaux éléments comme une allée de santolines et de romarin et une chute d'eau en cascade.

El Castillo de Marqueyssac, un edificio del siglo XVII, ofrece unas espléndidas vistas panorámicas del valle de Dordoña. Se construyó por orden de Bertrand Vernet de Marqueyssac, un consejero de Luis XIV. En 1861, pasó por herencia a Julien de Cerval, un apasionado de los jardines que había vivido un tiempo en Italia. Diseñó de nuevo el conjunto de jardines con terrazas y mandó plantar más de 150.000 árboles de boj, tallados con unas formas redondeadas fantásticas. A partir de 1996, Kléber Rossillon, el nuevo propietario, restauró los jardines que conservaron su antiguo aspecto. Añadió asimismo nuevos elementos, como un sendero de santolina y romero, y una cascada.

Giverny
Haute-Normandie, France

In 1890, the artist Claude Monet bought this land and set about creating the gardens that would become the subject of some of his most famous paintings. Inspired by tranquil scenes from Japanese prints that he collected, the garden has two distinct halves: the Flower Garden, where Monet combined daisies and poppies with the rarest species of flowers and trained climbers over an extensive network of iron frames; and the Water Garden, featuring a pool that mirrors the water lilies, willows and the Japanese Bridge. The house and gardens became a museum open to the public in 1980.

Im Jahr 1890 kaufte der Künstler Claude Monet dieses Land und schickte sich an, jene Gärten zu gestalten, die ihm als Motiv für einige seiner wohl berühmtesten Gemälde dienen sollten. Inspiriert von den friedvollen Szenen japanischer Drucke, die der Meister zu sammeln pflegte, teilt sich der Garten in zwei unterschiedliche Hälften: den Blumengarten, wo Monet Gänseblümchen und Mohnblumen mit seltensten Blumenarten kombinierte und Kletterpflanzen über weitläufige Eisengerüste wachsen ließ; und den Wassergarten, wo sich Seerosen, Weiden und eine japanische Brücke im Teich spiegeln. 1980 wurden das Haus und die Gärten in ein öffentlich zugängliches Museum umgewandelt.

En 1890, l'artiste Claude Monet, après avoir acquis un terrain dans la commune, y a aménagé le jardin qu'il a par la suite peint dans certaines de ses toiles parmi les plus célèbres. Inspiré de la sérénité des estampes japonaises qu'il collectionnait, le jardin se divise en deux parties bien distinctes : le jardin de fleurs dans lequel Monet a combiné marguerites et coquelicots avec des espèces florales plus rares et fait pousser des plantes grimpantes sur une large structure d'armature en fer ; et le jardin d'eau et son bassin dans lequel se reflète les nénuphars, les saules pleureurs et le pont japonais. La maison et le jardin forment désormais un musée ouvert au public depuis 1980.

En 1890, el artista Claude Monet adquirió este terreno y decidió crear los jardines que se convertirían en el tema de algunos de sus cuadros más famosos. El jardín, inspirado en las apacibles escenas de las estampas japonesas que el pintor coleccionaba, consta de dos partes muy distintas: el Jardín de Flores, donde Monet combinaba margaritas y amapolas con las especies más raras de flores y enredaderas adiestradas sobre una extensa trama de estructuras de hierro, y el Jardín de Agua, con un estanque en el que se reflejan nenúfares, sauces llorones y el Puente japonés. La casa y los jardines se convirtieron en un museo abierto al público en 1980.

Giverny, Haute-Normandie, France

Gardens of Versailles
Île-de-France, France

The greatest of baroque formal gardens, the Gardens of Versailles, situated to the west of the palace, cover some 800 hectares of land, much of which was landscaped by André Le Nôtre under the orders of Louis XIV. The gardens are now one of the most visited public sites in France, receiving more than six million visitors a year. In addition to the fastidiously manicured lawns, parterres of flowers, and the sculptures, are the truly spectacular fountains, for which the gardens are famed. The original network of hydraulics is still used to jet water across the spectacular views for visitors. In 1979, Versailles was declared a UNESCO World Heritage site.

Die Gärten von Versailles sind die größten aller barocken Formalgärten. Sie liegen im Westen des Schlosses und erstrecken sich über eine Fläche von ungefähr 800 Hektar, die zu einem großen Teil von André Le Nôtre im Auftrag Ludwig XIV. gestaltet wurden. Mit über sechs Millionen Besuchern pro Jahr zählen die Gärten heute zu den meistbesichtigten öffentlichen Orten Frankreichs. Neben den penibel gepflegten Rasenflächen, Blumen-parterres und Skulpturen sind die Gärten in erster Linie für ihre atemberaubend spektakulären Brunnen berühmt. Das ursprüngliche Bewässerungssystem dient auch heute noch dazu, die eindrucksvollen Ansichten vor den Augen der Besucher mit Wasser zu besprenkeln. Im Jahr 1979 wurde Versailles von der UNESCO zum Weltkulturerbe erklärt.

Plus grands jardins de style baroque, les jardins du château de Versailles, aménagés dans l'aile occidentale du palace, s'étendent sur quelques 800 hectares de terrain, dont la majeure partie a été arrangée par André Le Nôtre sous les ordres de Louis XIV. Les jardins figurent aujourd'hui parmi les sites publics les plus visités de France et accueillent plus de six millions de visiteurs par an. Outre les pelouses soigneusement entretenues, les parterres de fleurs et les sculptures, les jardins sont surtout connus pour leurs fontaines et le formidable spectacle qu'elles offrent. Le système hydraulique d'origine fait toujours fonctionner le ballet de jets d'eau pour le plus grand émerveillement des visiteurs. Versailles a été classé au patrimoine mondial de l'UNESCO en 1979.

Los Jardines de Versalles, los mejores jardines barrocos de diseño formal, se encuentran al oeste del palacio y abarcan unas 800 hectáreas de tierra, gran parte de las cuales fueron diseñadas por André Le Nôtre, siguiendo las órdenes de Louis XIV. Los jardines son ahora uno de los lugares públicos más visitados de Francia, con más de seis millones de visitantes al año. Además de las esculturas, y del césped y los parterres de flores cuidados con sumo esmero, son sus espectaculares fuentes las que dan fama a estos jardines. Aún se sigue utilizando la red hidráulica original para los surtidores de agua que proporcionan unas magníficas vistas a los visitantes. En 1979, Versalles fue declarado Patrimonio de la Humanidad de la UNESCO.

Parc de Joan Miró
Barcelona, Spain

Parc de Joan Miró, also known as El Parc de l'Escorxador, is a vast urban space, located on the former site of a municipal slaughterhouse. The public park, which is laid out over two levels, is the work of four local architects and covers four city blocks, offering lots of space to the locals and tourists who visit it. The intimate lower level is landscaped with pines, palms and eucalyptus trees, while the upper level is paved and features the park's most famous attraction, Miró's colourful sculpture entitled 'Dona i Ocell' ('Woman and Bird').

Der auch als Parc de l'Escorxador bekannte Parc de Joan Miró erstreckt sich über ein weitläufiges urbanes Gebiet und befindet sich auf dem Gelände eines ehemaligen städtischen Schlachthofes. Der auf zwei Ebenen angelegte öffentliche Park wurde von vier lokalen Architekten geschaffen und bietet Einheimischen und Touristen auf einer Fläche von vier Häuserblocks ausreichend Platz. Die innige untere Ebene wurde mit Pinien, Palmen und Eukalypten bepflanzt, während die obere Ebene gepflastert ist und die berühmteste Sehenswürigkeit des Parks beherbergt, Mirós farbenprächtige Skulptur namens „Dona i Ocell" („Frau und Vogel").

Le parc Joan-Miró, également connu sous le nom de Parc de l'Escorxador (parc des Abattoirs), est un vaste espace urbain situé sur le site d'anciens abattoirs municipaux. Le parc public aménagé sur deux niveaux est le fruit de quatre architectes locaux et couvre quatre pâtés d'habitations, offrant ainsi beaucoup d'espaces verts aux résidents comme aux touristes. Arboré de pins, de palmiers et d'eucalyptus, le niveau inférieur propose une ambiance intimiste alors que le niveau supérieur, entièrement pavé, expose l'attraction la plus célèbre du parc, la sculpture colorée de Miró baptisée « Dona i Ocell » (« Femme et oiseau »).

El Parque de Joan Miró, conocido igualmente como *El Parc de l'Escorxador*, es un extenso espacio urbano que se encuentra en el antiguo emplazamiento de un matadero municipal. El parque público, situado en dos niveles, es obra de cuatro arquitectos locales y ocupa el espacio de cuatro manzanas urbanas. Ofrece numerosos espacios a los lugareños y turistas que lo visitan. El nivel inferior, de carácter más íntimo, está lleno de pinos, palmeras y eucaliptos, mientras que el superior, pavimentado, presenta la atracción más famosa del parque: la colorida escultura de Miró «Dona i Ocell» («Mujer y Pájaro»).

Set high in the 19th arrondissement, Parc des Buttes-Chaumont is one of Paris's most romantic spots. When the city's boundaries were expanded in 1860, the Belleville area was absorbed and this park was created on the site of a former gypsum and limestone quarry. Designed by Jean-Charles Adolphe Alphand for Baron Haussmann, the park, with its spectacular rocky cliff sculpted by dynamite, its sinuous paths and its waterfalls, was opened for the Universal Exhibition in 1867. Its most famous feature is the Temple de la Sibylle, inspired by the Temple of Vesta in Tivoli, Italy.

Der im äußersten Nordosten des 19. Arrondissements gelegene Parc des Buttes-Chaumont ist zweifelsfrei einer der romantischsten Orte in ganz Paris. Bei der Erweiterung der Stadtgrenzen im Jahr 1860 wurde das Stadtviertel von Belleville eingemeindet und entstand dieser Park am ehemaligen Gelände eines Gips- und Kalksteinbruchs. Der von Adolphe Alphand für den Baron Haussmann entworfene Park mit seiner unter Zuhilfenahme von Dynamit geformten Felswand, seinen geschwungenen Pfaden und Wasserfällen wurde im Rahmen der Weltausstellung im Jahr 1867 eröffnet. Seine wohl berühmteste Sehenswürdigkeit ist der am Tempel der Vesta im italienischen Tivoli angelehnte Temple de la Sibylle oder Sibyllentempel.

Sur les hauteurs du 19ème arrondissement, le Parc des Buttes-Chaumont est l'un des sites les plus romantiques de Paris. Dans le cadre des réalisations urbaines initiées en 1860, la commune de Belleville fut annexée à Paris, et ce parc fut aménagé sur le site d'une ancienne carrière d'extraction de gypse et de pierres meulières. Conçu par Adolphe Alphand pour le Baron Haussmann, le parc et ses spectaculaires escarpements rocheux sculptés à la dynamite, ses sentiers sinueux et ses cascades, fut inauguré pour l'Exposition universelle en 1867. Le parc est célèbre pour son Temple de la Sibylle, inspiré du Temple de Vesta à Tivoli en Italie.

Situado en la cima del distrito 19, el Parque de Buttes-Chaumont es uno de los lugares más románticos de París. En 1860, al ampliarse los límites de la ciudad, la zona de Belleville quedó absorbida y se creó este parque en el emplazamiento de una antigua cantera de yeso y piedra caliza. Diseñado por Adolphe Alphand para el Barón Haussmann, el parque, con su espectacular acantilado rocoso esculpido mediante dinamita, sus sinuosos senderos y cascadas, se inauguró para la Exposición Universal de 1867. Su rasgo más característico es el *Temple de la Sibylle*, inspirado en el Templo de Vesta de Tívoli, Italia.

Keukenhof
Lisse, The Netherlands

Wohl niemand käme auf den Gedanken, Keukenhof, zu Deutsch „Küchengarten", Bescheidenheit oder unzureichende Ambitionen nachzusagen. Zwar wurde der weltgrößte Blumengarten im 15. Jahrhundert von Jakobäa, der Gräfin von Holland, angelegt, um darin Obst und Gemüse zu ziehen. Jedoch stellt Keukenhof heute eine ganze Reihe verschiedener Gartenstile zur Schau, beispielsweise anhand eines englischen Landschaftsgartens, eines Naturgartens sowie eines japanischen Gartens, in dem alljährlich sieben Millionen Blumenzwiebeln gepflanzt werden. Die in den umliegenden Feldern büschelweise wachsenden Tulpen, Narzissen und Krokusse bieten Gartenbesuchern zudem bezaubernde und freudige Aussichten.

No one could accuse Keukenhof, meaning 'kitchen garden', of being lowly or domestic. The world's largest flower garden was created in the fifteenth century by the Countess of Holland, Jacoba van Beieren, for growing fruit and vegetables. Today, there are a variety of garden styles on display, including an English landscape garden, a nature garden, and a Japanese garden, in which 7 million flower bulbs are planted annually. The huge blocks of tulips, daffodils and crocuses growing in the neighbouring fields provide engaging and joyful views from the gardens.

On ne saurait reprocher au Keukenhof, qui signifie « jardin potager » en français, son côté rustique ou encore familial. Le plus grand jardin floral du monde a été conçu au quinzième siècle par la Comtesse de Hollande, Jacoba de Bavière, pour y faire pousser des fruits et des légumes. Le Keukenhof se décline aujourd'hui en une variété de styles différents, parmi lesquels un jardin paysager à l'anglaise, un jardin naturel et un jardin japonais, où sont plantés chaque année 7 millions de bulbes à fleurs. Les immenses champs de tulipes, de jonquilles et d'anémones dans le voisinage des jardins finissent de parfaire un tableau chatoyant aux notes colorées.

No se podría reprochar a Keukenhof, que significa «jardín de la cocina», de ser un jardín humilde o doméstico. El jardín de flores más grande del mundo fue creado en el siglo XV por la Condesa de Holanda, Jacoba van Beieren, para cultivar frutas y verduras. En la actualidad, se puede admirar una gran variedad de estilos de jardines, entre ellos, un jardín paisajístico inglés, un jardín natural y un jardín japonés, en los que se plantan anualmente unos siete millones de bulbos de flores. Las inmensas extensiones de tulipanes, narcisos y azafranes que crecen en los campos vecinos ofrecen unas alegres y atractivas vistas desde los jardines.

Originally laid out in the Dutch baroque style for William and Mary of Orange between 1686 and 1695, these gardens were transformed by Louis Napoleon around 1807 when the walls and stairways were replaced with an array of fine trees. Het Loo follows a strict symmetrical layout, typical of a seventeenth-century garden. The most distinguishing feature of the palace grounds are the parterres grouped around the central axis and planted with closely trimmed box hedges in decorative scroll patterns. The gardens as we see them today mostly date from the 1970s and early 1980s.

Die ursprünglich zwischen 1686 und 1695 für Wilhelm und Maria von Oranien im niederländischen Barockstil angelegten Gärten wurden um das Jahr 1807 im Namen Louis Napoléons umgestaltet, wobei Wände und Treppen durch eine Anzahl edler Bäume ersetzt wurden. Wie es für Gärten des 17. Jahrhunderts typisch ist, wurde die Anlage von Het Loo streng symmetrisch gegliedert. Das außergewöhnlichste Merkmal des Schlossparks sind die um eine zentrale Achse gruppierten und mit sauber gestutzen Buchsbaumhecken bepflanzten Parterres, die dekorative Schnörkelmuster bilden. Das heutige Erscheinungsbild der Gärten geht größtenteils auf die 1970er- und frühen 1980er-Jahre zurück.

Aménagés à l'origine dans le style baroque flamand pour Guillaume et Marie d'Orange entre 1686 et 1695, les jardins furent transformés par Louis Napoléon vers 1807 avec le remplacement des enceintes murales et des escaliers par un ensemble d'arbres majestueux. Het Loo obéit à une trame parfaitement symétrique caractéristique des jardins du dix-septième siècle. Les jardins du palais se distinguent notamment par leurs parterres regroupés autour d'un axe central et bordés de buis parfaitement taillés en spirales décoratives. Les jardins que l'on peut admirer aujourd'hui datent essentiellement des années 70 et du début des années 80.

Het Loo, Gelderland, The Netherlands

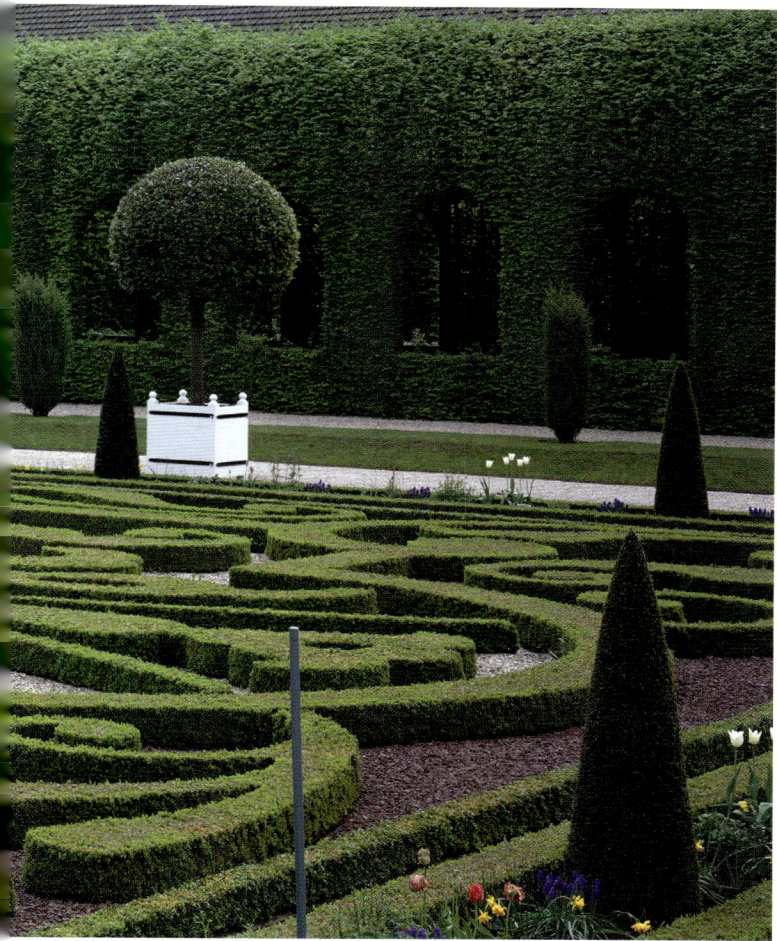

Creados, en origen, en estilo barroco holandés para Guillermo y María de Orange entre 1686 y 1695, los jardines se transformaron por orden de Luis Napoleón hacia 1807, cuando se sustituyeron paredes y escaleras por una fila de magníficos árboles. Het Loo sigue un estricto diseño simétrico, típico de un jardín del siglo XVII. El rasgo más característico del parque del palacio son los parterres agrupados en torno a un eje central y plantados con setos de boj rigurosamente recortados en decorativos motivos de volutas. Los jardines tal y como los apreciamos hoy en día datan, en su mayor parte, de la década de 1970 y de principios de los años 1980.

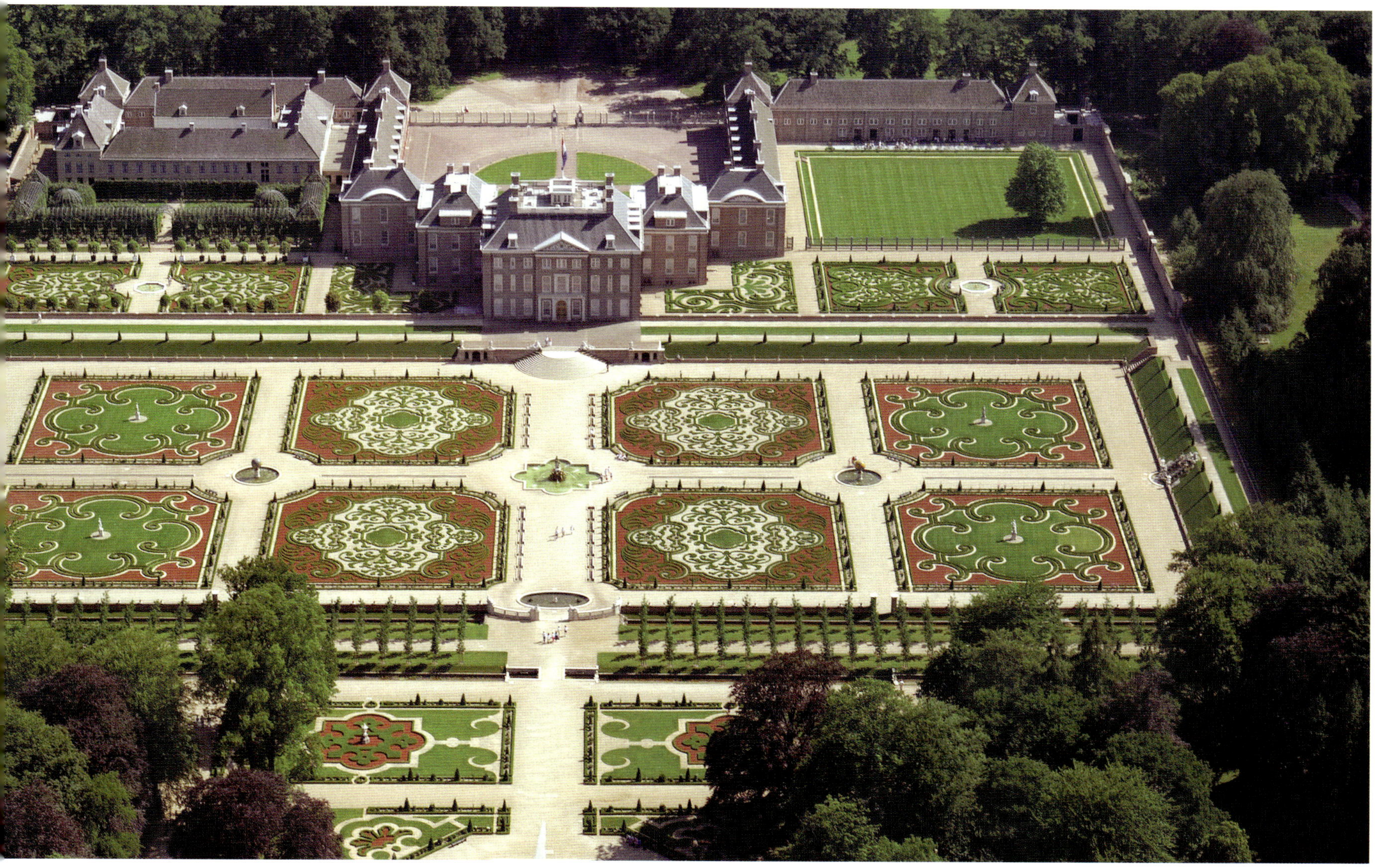

Isola Bella
Piedmont, Italy

Isola Bella is a small rocky island in Lake Maggiore. The palace and the terraced baroque gardens that slope to the lake were constructed on the barren rock in 1650 by Carlo III, from the noble Borromeo family, for his wife Isabella D'Adda, from whom the island gets its name. The cake-like structure of stone pillars and grottos is the defining feature of the dramatic gardens. The marble statues that adorn the top levels of the gardens gaze out at the beautiful views of the lake and the surrounding Alps.

Bei der Isola Bella handelt es sich um eine kleine felsige Insel inmitten des Lago Maggiore. Das Schloss und die zum See hin abfallenden terrassierten Barockgärten wurden im Jahr 1650 von Carlo III. Borromeo für seine Gemahlin Isabella D'Adda, nach der das Eiland schließlich benannt wurde, auf blankem Felsen errichtet. Die kuchenförmige Struktur aus Steinpfeilern und Grotten bildet das augenfälligste Merkmal der beeindruckenden Gärten. Die Marmorstatuen, welche die oberen Ebenen der Gärten zieren, scheinen sich an den atemberaubenden Aussichten auf den See und die umliegenden Alpen zu ergötzen.

Isola Bella est une petite île rocheuse sur le lac Majeur. Le palais et les jardins en terrasse de style baroque descendant en pente jusqu'au lac ont été construits sur les formations rocheuses en 1650 par le comte Charles III de la famille aristocratique Borromée pour sa femme Isabella d'Adda, dont l'île tire son nom. La structure en pièce montée formée par les piliers en pierre et les grottes caractérise ces jardins spectaculaires. Les statues de marbre qui ornent le sommet des jardins contemplent la vue sublime du lac en contrebas et des Alpes qui l'entourent.

Isola Bella es una pequeña isla rocosa situada en el Lago Mayor. El palacio y los jardines barrocos en bancales, que bajan hasta el lago, fueron construidos en una árida roca en 1650 por Carlos III, de la noble familia de los Borromeo, para su esposa Isabella D'Adda, de la que toma el nombre la isla. La estructura en forma piramidal de los pilares y las grutas de piedra es el rasgo más característico de estos espectaculares jardines. Las estatuas de mármol, que adornan los niveles superiores de los jardines, dirigen su mirada hacia las espléndidas vistas del lago y de los Alpes circundantes.

This naturalistic-style space was first established as a private garden over two hundred years ago, when it was acquired by the industrialist Freudenberg family in 1888. Between 1981 and 1983, it was radically overhauled by Hans Luz to make it the intimate and informal place it is today. The garden cultivates about 2,500 species, and in spring it is host to vast swathes of tulips. It also has a peony collection and a North American prairie garden, and many of the garden's trees, including a giant sequoia, date back to its very beginnings.

Schau- und Sichtungsgarten Hermannhof
Hessen, Germany

Este espacio, de estilo naturalista, se fundó primero como jardín privado hace más de doscientos años y, en 1888, fue adquirido por la familia de industriales Freudenberg. Entre 1981 y 1983, sufrió una renovación radical, llevada a cabo por Hans Luz, que lo convirtió en el lugar más íntimo e informal que es hoy en día. El jardín cultiva unas 2.500 especies y, en primavera, se adorna con grandes extensiones de tulipanes. Ofrece igualmente una colección de peonías y un jardín de pradera de América del Norte. Muchos de los árboles del jardín, incluida una secuoya gigante, datan de sus primeros tiempos.

Cet espace d'inspiration naturaliste a été à l'origine aménagé en tant que jardin privé sur plus de deux cents ans, après avoir été acquis par la famille d'industriels Freudenberg en 1888. Entre 1981 et 1983, le jardin a été totalement remanié par Hans Luz pour en faire l'espace intimiste et informel que l'on connaît aujourd'hui. Près de 2 500 espèces y sont cultivées, et au printemps, le jardin voit fleurir de larges bandes de tulipes. Il abrite également une collection de pivoines et un jardin reproduisant les prairies d'Amérique du Nord. Nombreux des arbres qui y sont plantés, y compris un séquoia géant, datent de son aménagement initial.

Ursprünglich wurde dieser Naturraum vor über zweihundert Jahren als Privatgarten kultiviert, bevor er im Jahr 1888 in den Besitz der Industriellenfamilie Freudenberg kam. Zwischen 1981 und 1983 wurde er von Hans Luz radikal umgestaltet und in den innigen und zwanglosen Ort verwandelt, der er heute ist. In diesem Garten werden ungefähr 2500 verschiedene Arten angebaut und im Frühling wachsen hier Tulpen in Hülle und Fülle. Des Weiteren verfügt das Anwesen über eine Sammlung an Strauchpäonien sowie einen nordamerikanischen Präriegarten. Ein guter Teil des Baumbestandes des Hermannshofes, darunter auch ein Mammutbaum, gehen zurück auf die Ursprünge dieses Gartens.

Frogner Park
Oslo, Norway

Der auch als Vigeland-Skulpturenpark bekannte Frogner Park ist die größte, von einem einzigen Künstler geschaffene Anlage dieser Art. Er beherbergt eine berühmte Sammlung von über 600 lebensgroßen Aktfiguren aus Bronze, Granit und Schmiedeeisen des norwegischen Bildhauers Gustav Vigeland. Die entlang einer 850 Meter langen Achse aufgereihten, anschaulichen und häufig humorvollen Skulpturen versinnbildlichen den Lebenszyklus von Geburt und Verfall bzw. von Familie und menschlichen Beziehungen. Sie scheinen den Betrachter geradezu dazu aufzufordern, an ihnen hochzuklettern und mit ihnen zu interagieren. Vigeland zeichnete auch für den Entwurf und die architektonische Gestaltung des zwischen 1939 und 1949 vollendeten neoklassizistischen Parks verantwortlich.

Frogner Park, also known as Vigeland Sculpture Park, is the world's largest of its kind by a single artist. It is home to a famous installation of over 600 full-size nude figures in bronze, granite and wrought iron by the Norwegian sculptor Gustav Vigeland. The graphic and often humorous sculptures, running along an 850-metre axis, depict the life cycle of birth and decay, family, and human relationships, and seem to invite visitors to climb onto and interact with them. Vigeland was also responsible for the design and architectural layout of the neoclassical park, completed between 1939 and 1949.

Le parc Frogner, également connu sous le nom de Parc Installation Vigeland, est le plus grand espace de ce type au monde conçu par un seul artiste. Il abrite un célèbre ensemble composé de plus de 600 sculptures de nus de pleine grandeur en bronze, granit et fer forgé du sculpteur norvégien Gustav Vigeland. Ses œuvres graphiques et souvent comiques dépeignent, le long d'un axe de 850 mètres, le cycle de la vie, de la naissance au déclin, la famille et les relations humaines, et semblent inviter le visiteur à venir les explorer et à interagir avec elles. Vigeland s'est également vu confier la conception et l'aménagement architectural du parc néoclassique. Commencés en 1939, les travaux ont été achevés en 1949.

El Parque Frogner, también conocido como Parque de Esculturas de Vigeland, es el mayor parque realizado por un único artista del mundo. Alberga una famosa instalación de más de 600 figuras desnudas de tamaño natural hechas de bronce, granito y hierro forjado, obra del escultor noruego Gustav Vigeland. Las esculturas gráficas, y a menudo humorísticas, dispuestas a lo largo de un eje de 850 metros, describen el ciclo vital del nacimiento al declive, así como las relaciones familiares y humanas. Parecen invitar a los visitantes a trepar e interactuar con ellas. Vigeland fue también el autor del diseño y la disposición arquitectónica del parque neoclásico, completado entre 1939 y 1949.

Villa Lante
Lazio, Italy

Beginning in 1568, the mannerist gardens at Villa Lante were designed for Cardinal Gianfrancesco Gambara by the architect Giacomo Barozzi da Vignola. The geometrical gardens revolve around a main axis which divides the twin houses of the villa and lends the gardens a spectacular symmetry. Engineer Tommaso Ghinucci was brought in to provide the hydraulic knowledge necessary to create the cascades, complex fountains and grottos that adorn the four terraces. Following the demise of the villa's last cardinal, the property was passed on to the family of Duke Ippolito Lante, from whom it gets its current name.

Beginnend mit dem Jahr 1568 wurden die manieristischen Gärten der Villa Lante vom Architekten Giacomo Barozzi da Vignola im Auftrag Kardinals Gianfrancesco Gambara angelegt. Die geometrischen Gärten liegen zu beiden Seiten einer Hauptachse, welche die Zwillingsbauten der Villa voneinander trennt und den Gärten eine spektakuläre Symmetrie verleiht. Der Architekt Tommaso Ghinucci wurde gerufen, um dank seiner Fachkenntnisse die Errichtung jener Kaskaden, komplexen Brunnen und Grotten zu ermöglichen, welche die vier Terrassen zieren. Nach dem Ableben des letzten hier residierenden Kardinals ging das Anwesen in den Besitz der herzöglichen Familie Ippolito Lantes über, wodurch die Villa zu ihrem heutigen Namen kam.

Villa Lante, Lazio, Italy

En 1568, el arquitecto Giacomo Barozzi da Vignola diseñó los jardines manieristas de la Villa Lante para el cardenal Gianfrancesco Gambara. Los jardines geométricos giran en torno a un eje principal que separa las dos casas idénticas de la villa y proporciona a los jardines una simetría espectacular. Se recurrió al ingeniero Tommaso Ghinucci a fin de que proporcionara los conocimientos hidráulicos necesarios para crear las cascadas, las complejas fuentes y las grutas que adornan las cuatro terrazas. Tras el fallecimiento del último cardenal de la villa, la propiedad pasó a la familia del duque Ippolito Lante, del que procede su nombre actual.

Débutés en 1568, les jardins maniéristes de la Villa Lante ont été dessinés en l'honneur du cardinal Gianfrancesco Gambara par l'architecte Giacomo Barozzi da Vignola. Ces jardins géométriques se déploient autour d'un axe principal qui sépare les maisons jumelles de la villa et confère aux jardins cette symétrie parfaite. Les connaissances hydrauliques de l'ingénieur Tommaso Ghinucci ont été mises à profit pour créer les cascades, les fontaines complexes et autres grottes qui viennent ponctuer les quatre terrasses. Après le décès du dernier cardinal résidant dans la villa, la propriété fut léguée à la famille du duc Ippolito Lante, dont elle tire son nom actuel.

Home to one of the most impressive and flamboyant of Italy's High Renaissance gardens, Villa d'Este was built between 1560 and 1572 by Pirro Ligorio for Cardinal Ippolito II d'Este on the occasion of his gaining the position of Governor of Tivoli. The garden of this UNESCO World Heritage site is laid out along a central axis that runs up to the steep Hundred Fountains and a series of diagonal paths leading towards the villa. Inspired by examples from antiquity, Claude Venard constructed a water organ whose curious hydraulic music fills the gardens several times a day.

Villa d'Este
Tivoli, Italy

Die zwischen 1560 und 1572 von
Pirro Ligorio für Kardinal Ippolito II.
d'Este anlässlich dessen Ernennung
zum Stadthalter von Tivoli errichtete
Villa d'Este beherbergt einen der wohl
beeindruckendsten und auffälligsten
Gärten aus der Zeit der Hochrenaissance,
die Italien zu bieten hat. Der Garten
dieser UNESCO-Weltkulturerbestätte
wurde entlang einer Mittelachse angelegt,
welche steil zu den sogenannten
„Hundert Brunnen" sowie einer Reihe
von Querpfaden ansteigt, die zur Villa
hinführen. Claude Venard, der sich
an antiken Vorbildern inspirierte,
errichtete eine Wasserorgel, deren einzigartige hydraulische Musik mehrmals
am Tag den Garten erfüllt.

Abritant l'un des jardins de la haute
Renaissance italienne parmi les plus
saisissants et flamboyants du pays,
la Villa d'Este fut construite entre
1560 et 1572 par Pirro Ligorio pour le
cardinal Hippolyte II d'Este suite à
la nomination de ce dernier au poste
de gouverneur de Tivoli. Inscrit au
patrimoine mondial de l'UNESCO,
le jardin se déploie le long d'un axe
central que bordent les incroyables
Cents fontaines et se divise en une
série de sentiers en diagonale menant
jusqu'à la villa. S'inspirant des modèles
de l'antiquité, Claude Venard y con-
struisit un orgue d'eau dont la curieuse
musicalité hydraulique vient enchanter
le jardin plusieurs fois par jour.

La Villa de Este, que alberga uno de
los jardines más impresionantes y
exuberantes del Alto Renacimiento
de Italia, fue construida entre 1560 y
1572 por Pirro Ligorio para el cardenal
Hipólito II de Este, con ocasión de
su nuevo puesto de gobernador de
Tívoli. El jardín de este lugar declarado
Patrimonio de la Humanidad de
la UNESCO está dispuesto a lo largo
de un eje central que recorre las
empinadas Cien Fuentes y una serie
de sendas diagonales que llevan a
la villa. Inspirándose en ejemplos
de la Antigüedad, Claude Venard
construyó un órgano de agua cuya
curiosa música hidráulica llena de
armonía los jardines varias veces al día.

One of the most beautiful baroque gardens in Europe, the Mirabell Gardens were built along a north–south axis and oriented towards the Hohensalzburg Fortress and Salzburger Dom Cathedral. The basic layout of the parterres of the gardens dates from 1601, when the palace was first built, but the gardens were redesigned in 1690, and again around 1730 by Franz Anton Danreiter. They were opened to the public by Emperor Franz Joseph in 1854. Highlights include the Hedge Theatre; the Dwarf Garden, featuring a number of misshapen creatures made of white Untersberg marble, and the Pegasus Fountain.

Der Mirabellgarten zählt zu den schönsten Barockgärten Europas. Er wurde entlang einer Nord-Süd-Achse angelegt, die unmittelbar zur Festung Hohensalzburg und zum Salzburger Dom weist. Zwar geht die wesentliche Anlage der Parterres auf das Jahr 1601 zurück, und fällt so mit der Errichtung des Schlosses zusammen, jedoch wurden die Gärten zwei Mal einer Neugestaltung unterzogen, einmal im Jahr 1690 und ein weiteres Mal im Jahr 1730 durch Franz Anton Danreiter. 1854 wurde der Mirabellgarten von Kaiser Franz Joseph der Öffentlich zugänglich gemacht. Zu den Sehenswürigkeiten zählen das Heckentheater, der Zwergerlgarten, der eine Reihe ungestalter Geschöpfe aus weißem Untersberger Marmor umfasst, sowie der Pegasusbrunnen.

Figurant parmi les plus beaux jardins baroques d'Europe, les jardins Mirabell se déploient le long d'un axe nord-sud en direction de la forteresse d'Hohensalzburg et de la cathédrale Saint-Rupert de Salzbourg. L'aménagement original des parterres des jardins date de 1601, année de construction du château. Les jardins ont été redessinés en 1690 puis de nouveau vers 1730 par Franz Anton Danreiter. L'Empereur François-Joseph décida de les ouvrir au public en 1854. Le théâtre de haies, le jardin des nains et ses statues de personnages difformes en marbre blanc d'Untersberg et la fontaine de Pégase figurent parmi les incontournables de ces jardins.

Los Jardines de Mirabell, uno de los jardines barrocos más bellos de Europa, se construyeron a lo largo de un eje norte-sur y están orientados hacia la fortaleza de Hohensalzburg y la catedral de Salzburgo. El diseño básico de los parterres de los jardines data de 1601, cuando se construyó el palacio por primera vez, pero los jardines se volvieron a diseñar en 1690 y de nuevo en 1730, por Franz Anton Danreiter. El Emperador Francisco José los abrió al público en 1854. Entre los elementos más destacados se encuentran el Teatro Hedge, el Jardín Enano, que presenta algunas criaturas contrahechas de mármol blanco de Untersberg, y la Fuente de Pegaso.

Few botanical gardens can match the sheer grandeur of Kirstenbosch, set as it is on the eastern slopes of Cape Town's Table Mountain. Kirstenbosch National Botanical Garden was established in 1913, devoted to preserving the immense floral wealth of the Cape. More than 7,000 species are cultivated here, including many whose existence outside of the garden's boundaries is under threat. The garden, with its more than 200 hectares, is part of an estate and nature reserve in the heart of the Cape Floristic region, a UNESCO World Heritage site.

Kirstenbosch National Botanical Garden
Cape Town, South Africa

Was die schiere Herrlichkeit des Ortes anbelangt, so können nur sehr wenige botanische Gärten dem malerisch an den östlichen Ausläufern von Kapstadts Tafelberg gelegenen Kirstenbosch das Wasser reichen. Der botanische Garten Kirstenbosch wurde im Jahr 1913 mit dem Ziel ins Leben gerufen, den immensen Blumenreichtum des Kaps zu bewahren. Über 7000 Arten werden hier kultiviert, darunter zahlreiche Spezies, deren Fortbestand außerhalb der Gartenanlage bedroht ist. Der über 200 Hektar große botanische Garten ist Teil eines Anwesens und Naturschutzgebiets im Herzen der Florenregion Kapprovinz, die zum UNESCO-Weltkulturerbe gehört.

Rares sont les jardins botaniques à pouvoir rivaliser avec l'exceptionnelle majesté qui se dégage de Kirstenbosch, situé sur le flanc oriental de la montagne de la Table au Cap. Le jardin botanique national de Kirstenbosch a été créé en 1913 dans le but de préserver l'immense richesse florale du Cap. Plus de 7 000 espèces y sont cultivées, parmi lesquelles de nombreux spécimens dont la survie en dehors des frontières du jardin est menacée. Avec plus de 200 hectares, ce jardin fait partie d'une réserve naturelle nationale aménagée en plein cœur de la région floristique du Cap, site inscrit au patrimoine mondial de l'UNESCO.

173

Pocos jardines botánicos pueden
igualar la espectacular grandiosidad de
Kirstenbosch, situado como está en el
marco incomparable de las pendientes
orientales de la Montaña de la Mesa,
en Ciudad del Cabo. El Jardín Botánico
Nacional de Kirstenbosch, fundado en
1913, se dedica a conservar la inmensa
riqueza floral del Cabo. Aquí se cultivan
más de 7.000 especies, incluidas muchas
cuya existencia fuera de los límites del
jardín está amenazada. El jardín, con sus
más de 200 hectáreas, forma parte
de una propiedad y una reserva natural
en el corazón de la Región Floral de
Ciudad del Cabo, declarada Patrimonio
de la Humanidad de la UNESCO.

Nishat Bagh
Kashmir, India

Completed in 1633 by Prime Minister Asaf Khan, this Persian-style garden comprising twelve sprawling terraces representing the Zodiac signs became the subject of great envy from Khan's jealous son-in-law, Emperor Shah Jahan. The Emperor ordered the water supply to be cut off, but a loyal servant of Asaf Khan's bravely switched the water back on. Since then this 17-hectare garden in the Jammu and Kashmir state has flourished. It lies at the foot of the Zabarwan Mountains and offers spectacular views of Dal Lake. Nishat Bagh is best summed up by its Hindustani translation; simply put, it is a 'Garden of Delight'.

Dieser im Jahr 1633 von Premier-minister Asaf Khan vollendete Garten persischen Stils mit seinen zwölf weitläufigen Terrassen, welche die Tierkreiszeichen repräsentieren, erfüllte Kahns eifersüchtigen Schwiegersohn, den Großmogul Shah Jahan, mit unsagbarem Neid. Daraufhin befahl der Mogulkaiser, die Wasserzufuhr des Gartens zu unterbrechen, die jedoch von einem loyalen und überaus mutigen Untergebenen Asaf Khans wiederhergestellt wurde. Seitdem gedeiht dieser im Bundesstaat Jammu und Kashmir gelegene, 17 Hektar große Garten, der sich am Fuße des Zabarwan-Gebirges befindet und atemberaubende Aussichten auf den Dal-See bietet. Am besten lässt sich Nishat Bagh wohl mithilfe der Übersetzung seines Hindi-Namens beschreiben, der ganz einfach „Garten der Wonne" bedeutet.

Achevé en 1633 par le Premier ministre Asaf Khan, ce jardin, dans le plus pur style perse, se décline autour de douze terrasses majestueuses représentant chacune les signes du zodiaque. L'empereur Shâh Jahân, gendre d'Asaf Khan, aurait nourri à l'encontre de ce jardin une jalousie telle qu'il aurait ordonné d'en cesser tout arrosage. Un ordre courageusement transgressé par un loyal serviteur d'Asaf Khan, grâce auquel ce jardin de 17 hectares continue depuis de s'épanouir dans l'état de Jammu-et-Cachemire. Avec en toile de fond les montagnes Zabarwan, le jardin jouit d'une vue exceptionnelle sur le lac Dal. Le Nishat Bagh porte à merveille son nom qui, traduit de l'hindoustani, signifie en termes simples « Jardin de délice ».

Este jardín de estilo persa, finalizado en 1633 por el Primer Ministro Asaf Khan y con doce extensas terrazas que representan los signos del zodíaco, despertó una inmensa envidia en el resentido yerno de Khan, el Emperador Shah Jahan. A pesar de que el Emperador ordenó cortar el suministro de agua, un fiel sirviente de Asaf Khan, actuando con valentía, volvió a conectarla. Desde entonces, este jardín de 17 hectáreas ha florecido en el estado de Jammu y Cachemira. Situado al pie de los Montes Zabarwan, ofrece unas espectaculares vistas del Lago Dal. La mejor forma de resumir Nishat Bagh se refleja en su traducción del indostano, en pocas palabras, «jardín de la delicia».

The Taj Mahal, the famous marble mausoleum of the Mughal Dynasty, is set on a garden comprising neat rectangles of manicured lawn structured around the number four, or multiples of four, the holiest number in Islam. It is in the style of a charbagh garden, inspired by Persian gardens which were introduced to India by the first Mughal Emperor. The garden is divided into four parts, with two marble canals studded with fountains crossing in the centre. In each section, there are sixteen flowerbeds that have been divided by stone-paved raised pathways.

Das Taj Mahal, das berühmte Marmor-mausoleum der Mogul-Dynastie, liegt unmittelbar an einem Garten aus ordentlichen und gepflegten Rasenrechtecken, die rund um die Zahl Vier bzw. dem Vielfachen davon strukturiert sind, der heiligsten Zahl des Islam. Er wurde im Tschahār Bāgh- oder „Viergeteilter Garten"-Stil gestaltet, der sich an persischen Gärten inspiriert, und mit dem ersten Mogul-Kaiser Indien erreichte. Der Garten teilt sich in vier Teile, die von zwei in ein zentrales Brunnenbecken mündenden Marmorkanälen wiederum in zwei Hälften geschieden werden. In jedem Abschnitt befinden sich 16 Blumenbeete, die durch erhöhte und gepflasterte Pfade voneinander gertrennt sind.

El Taj Mahal, el famoso mausoleo de mármol de la dinastía mogola, se encuentra en medio de un jardín que presenta unos rectángulos compactos de un césped muy cuidado estructurados en torno al número cuatro, o múltiplos de cuatro: el número más sagrado del Islam. Está construido en el estilo de los jardines Charbagh, que se inspiran en los jardines persas introducidos en la India por el primer emperador mogol. El jardín está dividido en cuatro partes mediante dos canales de mármol, adornados con fuentes, que se cruzan en el centro. En cada sección, afloran dieciséis arriates separados por unos caminos pavimentados elevados.

Le Taj Mahal, célèbre mausolée de marbre de la dynastie Moghol, se dresse dans un jardin dont les pelouses parfaitement rectangulaires et soigneusement entretenues se déclinent autour du chiffre quatre ou de ses multiples, quatre étant un nombre sacré dans l'islam. Inspiré de la tradition du Chahar bagh et des jardins persans introduits en Inde par le premier empereur moghol, les jardins du Taj Mahal se divisent en quatre parties elles-mêmes démarquées par deux canaux en marbre ornés de fontaines à leur croisement. Chacune de ces parties se décomposent en seize parterres de fleurs dont les allées pavées légèrement surélevées délimitent les contours.

Taj Mahal
Uttar Pradesh, India

Conceived by Nongnooch Tansacha, the surreal and fantastical Nong Nooch Tropical Garden opened to the public in 1980 and is now a popular tourist attraction managed by Tansacha's son. Having purchased just under 250 hectares of rolling hills and valleys with her husband to use as a fruit plantation, in 1954 Nongnooch had a dramatic change of heart after a tour of Europe, where she was inspired by the many gardens she visited. The garden combines eastern and western features, and includes a formal cascade and abstract topiary, making these pleasure grounds a very special place indeed.

Der von Nongnooch Tansacha entworfene surrealistische bzw. fantastische Tropengarten Nong Nooch öffnete im Jahr 1980 seine Tore für die Allgemeinheit und bildet heute eine von Tansachas Sohn geführte und bei Touristen geschätzte Sehenswürdigkeit. Nachdem sie gemeinsam mit ihrem Ehemann 250 Hektar Land an geschwungenen Hügeln und sanften Talern erworben hatte, um darauf eine Obstplantage zu betreiben, vollzog sich bei Nongnooch ein dramtischer Sinneswandel, nachdem sie im Jahr 1954 Europa bereist und dabei zahlreiche Gärten besucht hatte, die ihr als Inspirationsquelle dienen sollten. Der Garten verbindet östliche und westliche Merkmale und bietet förmliche Kaskaden sowie abstrakte Formschnitte, was diese Lustanlage wahrlich zu einem einzigartigen Ort macht.

Aménagés par Nongnooch Tansacha, ces jardins tropicaux, surréalistes et fantastiques, ont été ouverts au public en 1980 et sont désormais une attraction touristique populaire gérée par le fils de Tansacha. Apres avoir achete 250 hectaresde vallons et vallées avec son époux pour en faire une plantation de fruits, Nongnooch a littéralement changé d'attitude après un séjour en Europe en 1954, un revirement largement inspiré par les nombreux jardins qu'elle a visités là-bas. Subtil mélange entre Occident et Orient, le jardin abrite une cascade traditionnelle associée à un art topiaire abstrait, conférant à ce lieu plaisant une aura réellement singulière.

Diseñado por Nongnooch Tansacha, el Jardín Tropical de Nong Nooch, con un toque fantástico y surrealista, se abrió al público en 1980. Se ha convertido actualmente en una popular atracción turística gestionada por el hijo de Tansacha. Tras adquirir, junto con su esposo, 250 hectáreas de ondulantes colinas y valles para utilizarlos como plantación de frutales, en 1954 Nongnooch cambió drásticamente de idea después de realizar un viaje por Europa, donde se inspiró en los numerosos jardines que visitó. El jardín, que combina características orientales y occidentales, incluye una cascada de diseño formal y un jardín topiario abstracto, que hacen de estos terrenos de recreo un lugar realmente muy especial.

Gardens by the Bay
Singapore

Gardens by the Bay is a vast park in central Singapore, consisting of three waterfront gardens. It was built as part of the government's initiative to improve the quality of life in the city-state by developing green and open spaces. The most astounding feature of the gardens are undoubtedly the 'Supertrees' which are home to enclaves of unique and exotic ferns and vines. There is an elevated walkway between two of the larger supertrees which allows visitors to enjoy an aerial view of the gardens. At night, the Supertrees come alive with a light and music show called the 'Garden Rhapsody'.

Bei den Gardens by the Bay handelt
es sich um einen weitläufigen Park
im Herzen Singapurs, der aus drei
Ufergärten besteht. Er wurde als Teil
einer Regierungsinitiative errichtet,
die zum Ziel hatte, die Lebensqualität
im Stadtstaat durch die Anlage von
Grünflächen und Naturräumen zu
verbessern. Das erstaunlichste Merkmal
der Gärten sind zweifelsohne ihre
„Superbäume", die einzigartigen Farnen
und Rankengewächsen als Zuhause
dienen. Zwischen zwei der größeren
Superbäume hindurch verläuft ein
erhöhter Flanierweg, der es Besuchern
ermöglicht, die Gärten aus der Vogel-
perspektive zu bestaunen. In der Nacht
erwachen die Superbäume in einer
Licht- und Musikshow zum Leben,
der sogenannten Garten-Rhapsodie.

Gardens by the Bay est un vaste parc en plein centre de Singapour décliné autour de trois jardins en bord de mer. Ces jardins ont été conçus dans le cadre d'une initiative lancée par le gouvernement dans le but d'améliorer la qualité de vie de la ville-état en développant des espaces verts et publics. Les futuristes arbres géants ou « supertrees » en constituent sans nul doute l'élément le plus surprenant. Ces structures servent d'abri à de nombreuses fougères et autres plantes grimpantes uniques et exotiques. Deux de ces arbres artificiels, parmi les plus imposants du parc, sont reliés par une passerelle qui permet au visiteur de profiter de la vue panoramique sur les jardins. De nuit, les arbres géants prennent vie en s'habillant de lumière au son d'un spectacle musical baptisé « Garden Rhapsody ».

Gardens by the Bay constituye' un extenso parque, en el centro de Singapur, compuesto por tres jardines frente a la costa. Se construyeron como parte de una iniciativa gubernamental para mejorar la calidad de vida de la ciudad-estado mediante el desarrollo de espacios verdes y abiertos. El rasgo más sobresaliente de los jardines son indudablemente los «superárboles» que acogen unos enclaves de helechos y enredaderas únicos y exóticos. Una pasarela elevada entre dos de los superárboles más grandes permite a los visitantes disfrutar de una sensacional vista aérea de los jardines. De noche, los superárboles cobran vida con un espectáculo de luces y música llamado *La Rapsodia del Jardín*.

Photography Credits

Yu Yuan
- p. 10/1 — Getty Images / De Agostini / W. Buss
- p. 12/3 — Getty Images / Pan Hong
- p. 14 — National Geographic
- p. 15 — Getty Images / Iain Masterton

Changdeokgung
- p. 16/7 — Getty Images
- p. 18 — National Geographic
- p. 19 — National Geographic
- p. 20 — National Geographic
- p. 21 — National Geographic

Namba Parks
- p. 22 — Jerde
- p. 23 — Jerde
- p. 24 — Jerde
- p. 25 — Jerde
- p. 26 — Jerde
- p. 27 — Jerde

Kenroku-en
- p. 28/9 — shutterstock
- p. 30 — Darby Sawchuk
- p. 31 — Darby Sawchuk

Rikugi-en
- p. 32 — shutterstock
- p. 33 — shutterstock

Royal Botanic Gardens Melbourne
- p. 34/5 — Shutterstock

Chinese Gardens of Friendship
- p. 36 — National Geographic
- p. 37 — shutterstock
- p. 38 — National Geographic
- p. 39 — National Geographic

Butchart Gardens
- p. 40 — Getty Images / Lisa Kling
- p. 41 — Getty Images / Dave Blackey
- p. 42 — Getty Images / Barrett & MacKay
- p. 43 — Getty Images / Barrett & MacKay
- p. 44/5 — Getty Images / Barrett & MacKay

Desert Botanical Gardens
- p. 46 — Desert Botanical Gardens
- p. 47 — Desert Botanical Gardens
- p. 48 — Desert Botanical Gardens
- p. 49 — Desert Botanical Gardens

Las Pozas
- p. 50 — National Geographic
- p. 51 — National Geographic
- p. 52 — National Geographic
- p. 53 — Getty Images / 183177280

Minneapolis Sculpture Garden
- p. 54 — © Design Pics Inc. / Alamy
- p. 55 — © Andriy Kravchenko / Alamy

Chicago City Hall
- p. 56 — National Geographic
- p. 57 — National Geographic
- p. 58 — National Geographic
- p. 59 — National Geographic

Museo Subacuático de Arte
- p. 60 — © Jason deCaires Taylor. All right reserved, DACS 2013
- p. 61 — © Jason deCaires Taylor. All right reserved, DACS 2013
- p. 62/3 — © Jason deCaires Taylor. All right reserved, DACS 2013
- p. 64 — © Jason deCaires Taylor. All right reserved, DACS 2013
- p. 65 — © Jason deCaires Taylor. All right reserved, DACS 2013

Central Park
- p. 66/7 — National Geographic
- p. 68 — National Geographic
- p. 69 — Getty Images / Chris Cor

High Line
- p. 70/1 — National Geographic
- p. 72 — National Geographic
- p. 73 — National Geographic

Jardin botanique de Montréal
- p. 74/5 — Jardin botanique de Montréal (by Claude Lafond)
- p. 76 — Getty Images / Toshio Kishiyama
- p. 77 — Getty Images / Renault Philippe / hemis.fr

Gilberto Strunk Residence
- p. 78 — Jerry Harpur
- p. 79 — Jerry Harpur

Jardin Majorelle
- p. 80/1 — Getty Images / itsabreezephotography
- p. 82 — Getty Images / Kelly Cheng Travel Photography
- p. 83 — Getty Images / Kevin Button
- p. 84 — Getty Images / Jen Pollack Bianco
- p. 85 — Getty Images / Jen Pollack Bianco

National Botanic Gardens, Glasnevin
- p. 86/7 — © Design Pics Inc. – RM Content / Alamy
- p. 88 — shutterstock
- p. 89 — shutterstock

Powerscourt
- p. 90 — Powerscourt Estate
- p. 91 — National Geographic
- p. 92/3 — Powerscourt Estate

The Lost Gardens of Heligan
- p. 94/5 — shutterstock
- p. 96 — The Lost Gardens of Heligan
- p. 97 — The Lost Gardens of Heligan
- p. 98 — Tracy Packer
- p. 99 — TheLost Gardens of Heligan

Eden Project
- p. 100/1 — National Geographic
- p. 102/3 — National Geographic
- p. 104 — Getty Images / Jose Moya
- p. 105 — Getty Images / David Cayless

Bodnant Garden
- p. 106/7 — Getty Images / Brian Lawrence
- p. 108 — shutterstock
- p. 109 — shutterstock

Drummond Castle
- p. 110 — Ray Cox
- p. 111 — Ray Cox
- p. 112/3 — Ray Cox
- p. 114 — Ray Cox
- p. 115 — Ray Cox

Royal Botanic Gardens, Kew
- p. 116 — Getty Images / Horst Friedrichs
- p. 117 — National Geographic
- p. 118/9 — Getty Images / Chris Mellor
- p. 120 — National Geographic
- p. 121 — National Geographic

Château de Villandry
- p. 122/3 — Jerry Harpur
- p. 124 — Jerry Harpur
- p. 125 — Jerry Harpur

Château de Marqueyssac
- p. 126 — Laugery-Les Jardins de Marqueyssac-Dordogne
- p. 127 — Laugery-Les Jardins de Marqueyssac-Dordogne

Giverny
- p. 128/9 — Jerry Harpur
- p. 130 — Jerry Harpur
- p. 131 — Jerry Harpur

Gardens of Versailles
- p. 132/3 — Toucan Wings
- p. 134 — Toucan Wings
- p. 135 — Toucan Wings

Parc de Joan Miró
- p. 136 — Shutterstock
- p. 137 — Age fotostock Spain, S.L. / Alamy

Parc des Buttes-Chaumont
- p. 138/9 — shutterstock
- p. 140 — shutterstock
- p. 141 — shutterstock

Keukenhof
- p. 142 — Keukenhof Lentepark
- p. 143 — Keukenhof Lentepark
- p. 144 — Keukenhof Lentepark
- p. 145 — Keukenhof Lentepark

Het Loo
- p. 146/7 — Getty Images / Hollandluchtfoto
- p. 148 — National Geographic
- p. 149 — See Holland

Isola Bella
- p. 150/1 — Getty Images / Ken Welsh
- p. 152 — National Geographic
- p. 153 — National Geographic

Schau- und Sichtungsgarten Hermannhof
- p. 154/5 — Jerry Harpur
- p. 156 — Jerry Harpur
- p. 157 — Jerry Harpur

Frogner Park
- p. 158 — © Jeff Gilbert / Alamy
- p. 159 — © Prisma Bildagentur AG

Villa Lante
- p. 160 — Getty Images / Grahame McConnell
- p. 161 — © Andrea Jones / Alamy
- p. 162/3 — Getty Images / Michael Newton

Villa d'Este
- p. 164 — National Geographic
- p. 165 — shutterstock

Mirabellgarten
- p. 166/7 — shutterstock
- p. 168 — shutterstock
- p. 169 — shutterstock

Kirstenbosch National Botanical Garden
- p. 170/1 — National Geographic
- p. 172 — National Geographic
- p. 173 — Getty Images / Don Bailey

Nishat Bagh
- p. 174 — Getty Images / Exotica.m
- p. 175 — Getty Images / Uniquely India
- p. 176/7 — Getty Images / Exotica.m

Taj Mahal
- p. 178/9 — National Geographic

Nong Nooch Tropical Garden
- p. 180/1 — Getty Images / Frank Waldecker
- p. 182 — shutterstock
- p. 183 — shutterstock

Gardens by the Bay
- p. 184/5 — Far East Organization Children's Garden, Gardens by the Bay
- p. 186 — Far East Organization Children's Garden, Gardens by the Bay
- p. 187 — Far East Organization Children's Garden, Gardens by the Bay
- p. 188 — Far East Organization Children's Garden, Gardens by the Bay

124° E

136° E

148° E

117° W

97° W

87° W

74° W

WEST

PACIFIC
OCEAN

22
Namba Parks
OSAKA

34
Royal Botanic
Gardens
Melbourne
MELBOURNE

40
Butchart
Gardens
BRITISH
COLUMBIA

50
Las Pozas
SAN LUIS
POTOSÍ

56
Chicago
City Hall
ILLINOIS

66
Central Park
NEW YORK

10
Yu Yuan
SHANGHAI

28
Kenroku-en
ISHIKAWA

70
High Line
NEW YORK

16
Changdeokgung
SEOUL

36
Chinese Garden
of Friendship
NEW SOUTH
WALES

46
Desert Botanical
Garden
ARIZONA

54
Minneapolis
Sculpture
Garden
MINNESOTA

60
Museo
Subacuático
de Arte
CANCÚN

32
Rikugi-en
TOKYO

74
Jardin botanique
de Montréal
MONTREAL